Lessons of War

*Lincoln's Second Inaugural Address,
Leadership at Gettysburg*

Glen Aubrey

www.LessonsOfWar.com
www.ctrg.com

Creative Team Publishing
San Diego
www.CreativeTeamPublishing.com

© 2011 by Glen Aubrey.

All rights reserved. No part of this book may be reproduced, stored in a retrieval system or transmitted in any form or by any means without the prior written permission of the publisher, except by a reviewer who may quote brief passages in a review to be distributed through electronic media, or printed in a newspaper, magazine or journal.

ISBN: 978-0-9838919-7-0
PUBLISHED BY CREATIVE TEAM PUBLISHING
www.CreativeTeamPublishing.com
San Diego

Printed in the United States of America

Endorsements

Lessons of War—Lincoln's Second Inaugural Address, Leadership at Gettysburg is a tremendous contribution to the art and science of strategic leadership, as viewed through the crucible of human conflict. Glen Aubrey's insightful reflections into President Lincoln's Second Inaugural Address, particularly how Abraham Lincoln "set the conditions" for our nation's fateful transition from civil war to lasting peace, is critically relevant to the daunting challenges faced by our current senior political and military leaders, as they also determine how best to turn swords into plowshares in Iraq, Afghanistan, and beyond.
~ **Major General Robert F. Dees, United States Army, Retired, and Author of** *The Resilience Trilogy* **(www.ResilienceTrilogy.com, 2011)**

Many Americans have never encountered Lincoln's Second Inaugural Address, nor fully appreciate the strategic importance of the Battle of Gettysburg in our nation's history. Glen Aubrey's *Lessons of War—Lincoln's Second Inaugural Address, Leadership at Gettysburg* brings both of these historically significant events together in a poignant way. He helps us see clearly that seeking peaceful resolution is the ultimate aim of those forced to participate in war and that good leaders "choose the best ways to conduct and conclude it." Aubrey's insights are captivating and compelling. Examples of sound leadership lessons and principles abound in every chapter. Former, current and aspiring leaders would be wise to learn them, savor them...and apply them as they lead. This is a future classic.

~ **Colonel Barry E. Willey, United States Army, Retired, and Author of** *Out of the Valley* **(Officers' Christian Fellowship, 2007)**

With his clear and engaging style, Glen once again delivers a fascinating and indispensable examination of leadership, this time through the lens of an American hero. Lincoln's powerful legacy of strong leadership in war, founded upon his reverence for God, is a sterling model for every leader. Military and civilian leaders must apply the timeless lessons gleaned from Glen's analysis, particularly during this age of enduring conflict.

~ **Major Kevin Bouren, United States Army**

Leadership—real, enduring leadership—is shown in *Lessons of War—Lincoln's Second Inaugural Address, Leadership at Gettysburg* to be that which is firmly grounded in and based upon reality and truth, coupled with genuine caring for those being led. This, in turn, leads to the best preparation for and conduct of the conflict. Glen Aubrey carries forward these critical leadership principals, and shows how to succeed in the next and final phase of every conflict—the ending of the conflict, with an accompanying establishment of genuine peace, or as close to genuine peace as is humanly possible, and Godly allowed. A must read for anyone who wishes his or her own conflicts, personal or organizational, to end well.

~ Colonel John D. Kirby (Retired), United States Army, 1st Cavalry Division (Airmobile), Vietnam War Veteran; subsequently, Attorney-at-Law, Litigation

Abraham Lincoln often spoke of his religious beliefs when referring publicly to the purpose of the war, one to decide whether this nation, "so conceived and so dedicated, can long endure,"—a point so critical to the president and his constituents that he invoked God's name in two of his greatest speeches. Mr. Aubrey has compiled a narrative that delves deep into the role of religion in Lincoln's leadership and its influence in decision making among many of the war's highest ranking generals, both on and off the Civil War battlefield.

~ John Heiser, Historian, National Park Service, Gettysburg National Military Park

As an avid student of the nation-changing event we know as the Battle of Gettysburg, Glen Aubrey has now completed his second study of the lessons to be learned from that conflict and, more importantly, the lessons to be learned from studying the genius that was and is Abraham Lincoln. In *Lessons of War— Lincoln's Second Inaugural Address, Leadership at Gettysburg*, Glen opens our eyes to the message of hope, commitment, and faith in God that Lincoln so skillfully wove into his Second Inaugural Address. You cannot read this book without gaining enormous insight into Abraham Lincoln—the man. Glen then takes that insight and develops a clear understanding of how those truths can be used to enrich our own lives and leadership styles today.

~ Sergeant Stephen M. Annis, United States Air Force, Vietnam War Veteran 1966 – 1970; Executive Vice President and Chief Financial Officer, Valley Republic Bank

Permissions and Credits in Order of Appearance

Text of First Inaugural Address and text of Second Inaugural Address by Abraham Lincoln, quotes and proclamations, are in the public domain. Please see websites http://www.ourdocuments.gov and http://www.ourdocuments.gov/doc.php?flash=true&doc=38&page=transcript for transcript of the Second Inaugural Address.

Poetry selections "Division" "A Choice Away" "Beneath" are quoted From *Freedom Light—Expressions of Hope and Evidence* © 2009 Glen Aubrey. Used with permission.

References relating to costs of the Civil War are taken from websites http://www.civilwarhome.com/warcosts.htm, and http://www.civilwarhome.com, "Shotgun's Home of the American Civil War" First Published: January 7, 1997 by Webmaster: Dick *(a.k.a. Shotgun)*. Permission for use is granted: "If you simply need permission to use something on the site, feel free to use what you like."

The Three Days at Gettysburg written by John E. Pitzer, Gettysburg, PA., Member Post 9, G. A. R. (Grand Army of the Republic) and published by *"News" Press, Gettysburg, Pa.* circa 1900 is in the public domain.

Updated and corrected factual historical information is provided by John Heiser, Historian, National Park Service, Gettysburg National Military Park. Used with permission.

Quotes from *Lincoln, Leadership and Gettysburg* by Glen Aubrey, © 2009. Used with permission.

Account by General Joshua Chamberlain of his experiences with the 20th Maine Regiment on Little Round Top, published in *Hearst's Magazine* and reprinted by Stan Clark Military Books of Gettysburg, Pennsylvania, Copyright 1994. Used with permission.

Quotes from *Core Teams Work Their Principles and Practices* by Glen Aubrey, © 2007. Used with permission.

Quotes from *At Gettysburg or What a Girl Saw and Heard of the Battle—A True Narrative* written by Mrs. Tillie (Pierce) Alleman, new material copyrighted 1987, reprinted and distributed by Butternut and Blue, and Stan Clark Military Books, in 1994. Used with permission.

Story of Color Sergeant Ben Crippen: *The Historical Record, A Quarterly Publication Devoted Principally To The Early History of Wyoming Valley With Notes And Queries, Biographical, Antiquarian, Genealogical,* Edited by F. C. Johnson, M. D., Volume II, January 1888, No. 1, Wilkes-Barre, PA, Press of The Wilkes-Barre Record, MDCCCLXXXVIII is in the public domain.

Story of 1st Minnesota Infantry Regiment "The First Minnesota at Gettysburg. By Lieutenant William Lochren, First Minnesota Infantry, U. S. Volunteers., Read January 14, 1890." published in *Glimpses of the Nation's Struggle., Third Series., Papers Read Before The Minnesota Commandery of the Military Order of The Loyal Legion of the United States, 1889 – 1892,* Published for the Commandery, Chaplain Edward D. Neill, D.D., Editor., D. D. Merrill Company,

New York., St. Paul., Minneapolis., 1893., Copyright, 1893, D. D. Merrill Company is in the public domain.

The Holy Bible, King James Version (also known as the Authorized Version), 1611, is in the public domain.

Story of Ohio convention nominating John C. Frémont for President, from Clarence E. Macartney, *Lincoln and the Bible* (New York, 1949) is in the public domain and/or is used by permission of American Tract Society, http://www.atstracts.org/.

Quotation of Protest recorded in the Illinois Legislature on Slavery, March 3, 1837 from *House Journal*, Tenth General Assembly, First Session, pp. 817-818 is in the public domain.

Story of question to Lincoln whether God was on the side of the Union quoted from http://www.1-famous-quotes.com/quote/6352 for which permission is not required.

Civilian account quotation regarding Christ Lutheran Church used as a field hospital is in the public domain.

Story of Horatio Howell is used by permission of webmaster@stonesentinels.com.

Story of Sergeant Archibald B. Snow of the 97th New York Volunteers is in the public domain.

Leadership Is—How to Build Your Legacy, Copyright 2004 and 2011 by Glen Aubrey, published by Creative Team Publishing in 2011, quoting an edition of *Essays: First Series* (1841) by Ralph Waldo Emerson is used by permission of http://www.emersoncentral.com.

Word definitions from *Merriam-Webster's Collegiate Dictionary, Eleventh Edition.*

Story of Colonel Isaac Avery, North Carolina, National Park Service website, Gettysburg tour: http://www.nps.gov/archive/gett/getttour/tstops/tstd2-18.htm is in the public domain.

Story of meeting President and Mrs. George W. Bush, entitled "The Encounter" is quoted from *Industrial Strength Solutions Build Successful Work Teams!* by Glen Aubrey, Copyright 2006. Used with permission of PublishAmerica.

Quotation from Lieutenant-General Ulysses S. Grant, *Personal Memoirs of Ulysses S. Grant* (New York, 1885), pages 555-560 is in the public domain.

Story of High Street or "Common" School in Gettysburg used as a field hospital for both sides obtained from plaque positioned in front of the building. Signs were and are part of the Main Street Gettysburg Walking Interpretive Path. Permission to quote is not required.

Letters from the *Report of Lieut. Gen. Ulysses S. Grant, U. S. Army, commanding Armies of the United States, The Richmond (Virginia) Campaign from the Official Records of the War of the Rebellion, 1880-1901* are in the public domain.

Quotation of General P. G. T. Beauregard story, *The First Battle of Bull Run* published in *Battles and Leaders of the Civil War, Volume I, Being For The Most Part Contributions By Union And Confederate Officers., Based Upon "The Century War Series."*, Edited by Robert Underwood Johnson and Clarence Clough Buel, of the Editorial

Staff of "the Century Magazine.", New-York, The Century Co., Copyright, 1884-1887 By The Century Co." is in the public domain.

Robert E. Lee Address *Farewell to The Army of Northern Virginia, General Order No. 9* is in the public domain.

Quotation of Brig. General Joshua Chamberlain in *Passing of the Armies*, pages 260-261 is in the public domain.

Quotation from and reference to *The Last Reunion of the Blue and Gray*, written by Paul L. Roy, Gettysburg, Pennsylvania, copyrighted in 1950 by the author, published and distributed by The Bookmart of Gettysburg, Pennsylvania. Permission to quote is not required.

Text of speech of President Franklin Delano Roosevelt delivered at Gettysburg on July 3, 1938 is in the public domain.

Reference to Portable Document Format (pdf) of speech by President Franklin Delano Roosevelt at the 75th Reunion of Civil War veterans at Gettysburg, July 3, 1938 is used by permission of Bobby Housch, http://www.gettysburgdaily.com/files/speechofthepresident.pdf.

The Pledge of Allegiance to the flag of the United States is in the public domain.

Lyrics to "The Star-Spangled Banner" by Francis Scott Key, 1814 are in the public domain.

Disclaimer: Utmost due diligence was exercised to reference and obtain permission from all quoted sources. Where any source has inadvertently been listed inaccurately or information regarding sources listed as those for which permission was or was not required is shown to be incorrect, the publisher issues an apology and will correct any errors proven to be errors on the book's website: www.LessonsOfWar.com.

Lessons of War

Lincoln's Second Inaugural Address, Leadership at Gettysburg

Glen Aubrey

www.LessonsOfWar.com

Wars are part of the human experience.

We know we must enter them.

We know how to win them.

Let us learn how to end them well.

Table of Contents

Conflict and Resolution, War and Peace   21

Second Inaugural Address of President Abraham Lincoln, March 4, 1865   23

1   Deployment and Discovery   27
      "Division"   33

2   History Unites Us—Cause and Effect   37
      <u>Fellow Countrymen</u>

At this second appearing to take the oath of the Presidential office, there is less occasion for an extended address than there was at the first. Then a statement, somewhat in detail, of a course to be pursued, seemed fitting and proper. Now, at the expiration of four years, during which public declarations have been constantly called forth on every point and phase of the great contest which still absorbs the attention, and engrosses the energies of the nation, little that is new could be presented. The progress of our arms, upon which all else chiefly depends, is as well known to the public as to myself; and it is, I trust, reasonably satisfactory and encouraging to all. With high hope for the future, no prediction in regard to it is ventured.

3   Conflict Comes   47

On the occasion corresponding to this four years ago, all thoughts were anxiously directed to an impending civil-war. All dreaded it—all sought to avert it. While the inaugural address was being delivered from this place, devoted altogether to <u>saving</u> the Union without war, insurgent agents were in the city seeking to <u>destroy</u> it without war—seeking to dissolve the Union, and divide effects, by negotiation. Both parties deprecated war, but one of them would <u>make</u> war rather than let the nation survive; and the other would <u>accept</u> war rather than let it perish. And the war came.

One eighth of the whole population were colored slaves, not distributed generally over the Union, but localized in the Southern part of it. These slaves constituted a peculiar and powerful interest. All knew that this interest was, somehow, the cause of the war. To strengthen, perpetuate, and extend this interest was the object for which the insurgents would rend the Union, even by war; while the government claimed no right to do more than to restrict the territorial enlargement of it.

"A Choice Away"   55

4   The Unexpected Price of Winning   57

Neither party expected for the war, the magnitude, or the duration, which it has already attained. Neither anticipated that the <u>cause</u> of the conflict might cease with, or even before,

the conflict itself should cease. Each looked for an easier triumph, and a result less fundamental and astounding.
BY THE PRESIDENT OF THE UNITED STATES: A PROCLAMATION April 15, 1861   58

5   Belief and Practice—Faith Tried and Tested   67
Both read the same Bible, and pray to the same God; and each invokes His aid against the other. It may seem strange that any men should dare to ask a just God's assistance in wringing their bread from the sweat of other men's faces; but let us judge not that we be not judged. The prayers of both could not be answered; that of neither has been answered fully.

6   Offenses   77
The Almighty has His own purposes. "Woe unto the world because of offences! for it must needs be that offences come; but woe to that man by whom the offence cometh!" If we shall suppose that American Slavery is one of those offences which, in the providence of God, must needs come, but which, having continued through His appointed time, He now wills to remove, and that He gives to both North and South, this terrible war as the woe due to those by whom the offence came, shall we discern therein any departure from those divine attributes which the believers in a Living God always ascribe to Him?

7   Hope, Prayer, and Submission   85

Fondly do we hope—fervently do we pray—that this mighty scourge of war may speedily pass away. Yet, if God wills that it continue, until all the wealth piled by the bond-man's two hundred and fifty years of unrequited toil shall be sunk, and until every drop of blood drawn with the lash, shall be paid by another drawn with the sword, as was said three thousand years ago, so still it must be said "the judgments of the Lord, are true and righteous altogether."
Story of meeting President and Mrs. George W. Bush:
"The Encounter"   87

8   Firmness in the Right   97

With malice toward none; with charity for all; with firmness in the right, as God gives us to see the right…
Correspondence of Lieutenant-General Ulysses S. Grant and General Robert E. Lee, April 9, 1865, and Commentary   98

9   Finish the Work   109

…let us strive on to finish the work we are in; to bind up the nation's wounds; to care for him who shall have borne the battle, and for his widow, and his orphan—
Correspondence of Lieutenant-General Ulysses S. Grant and General Robert E. Lee beginning April 7, 1865, concluding April 9, 1865   110
Robert E. Lee Address *Farewell to The Army of Northern Virginia*, General Order No. 9   118

19

10   A Just and a Lasting Peace   123
    …to do all which may achieve and cherish a just, and a lasting peace, among ourselves, and with all nations. Speech of President Franklin Delano Roosevelt, July 3, 1938 at Gettysburg, the 75th Reunion of the Veterans of the Blue and Gray   124

One Nation under God   133
    The Pledge of Allegiance   133
    The Star-Spangled Banner   134
    "Beneath"   138

Bibliography   141
Acknowledgements   145

The Author   147
Creative Team Resources Group (CTRG)   149
Creative Team Publishing (CTP)   151
Books by Glen Aubrey   153
Music Audio Recordings by Glen Aubrey   155

Conflict and Resolution, War and Peace

Lessons of War—Lincoln's Second Inaugural Address, Leadership at Gettysburg relates conflict and resolution, war and peace. The Civil War (1861-1865) composed America's greatest trial since its founding. With the second inauguration of Abraham Lincoln on March 4, 1865 history would show that a little over a month remained until General Robert E. Lee would surrender to Lieutenant-General Ulysses S. Grant on April 9th, essentially bringing the conflict to a close. The war appeared to be ending so the president laid the framework for reconciliation of North and South in his inauguration address.

Many students of war know how conflict should be conducted. Many desire to learn how war should conclude. *Lessons of War— Lincoln's Second Inaugural Address, Leadership at Gettysburg* discovers profound leadership lessons embedded in Lincoln's Second Inaugural Address, and demonstrates how cessation of a conflict and eternal principles of reconciliation become standards of achievement when a war or a battle comes to a close. While Lincoln articulated these standards in his speech at the start of his second term, they had already been demonstrated at Gettysburg in 1863 as a part of that famous battle and its aftermath.

The battle of Gettysburg represented the supreme struggle of the Civil War, the turning point toward eventual victory for the Union. Lincoln's Second Inaugural Address represented the president's hope for final resolution of the conflict and a restoration of the country. Lincoln positioned high principles and practices into the national conscience in 1865, proving what had already been lived out at Gettysburg in 1863. Eventually the nation would be restored, though at the time no one could accurately predict when the Civil War would cease or what its final conclusion would be.

Wars are part of human history. While we may understand their causes and how to conduct them, we can learn from Lincoln and the examples of Gettysburg how to conclude them. Leaders, patriots, and peace lovers understand the value of ending conflicts well. These people of principle look to Lincoln's example. These individuals strive "*...to do all which may achieve and cherish a just, and a lasting peace, among ourselves, and with all nations.*"

Second Inaugural Address
Abraham Lincoln
March 4, 1865

<u>Fellow Countrymen</u>

 At this second appearing to take the oath of the Presidential office, there is less occasion for an extended address than there was at the first. Then a statement, somewhat in detail, of a course to be pursued, seemed fitting and proper. Now, at the expiration of four years, during which public declarations have been constantly called forth on every point and phase of the great contest which still absorbs the attention, and engrosses the energies of the nation, little that is new could be presented. The progress of our arms, upon which all else chiefly depends, is as well known to the public as to myself; and it is, I trust, reasonably satisfactory and encouraging to all. With high *hope for the future, no prediction in regard to it is ventured.*

On the occasion corresponding to this four years ago, all thoughts were anxiously directed to an impending civil-war. All dreaded it—all sought to avert it. While the inaugural address was being delivered from this place, devoted altogether to <u>saving</u> the Union without war, insurgent agents were in the city seeking to <u>destroy</u> it without war—seeking to dissolve the Union, and divide effects, by negotiation. Both parties deprecated war, but one of them would <u>make</u> war rather than let the nation survive; and the other would <u>accept</u> war rather than let it perish. And the war came.

One eighth of the whole population were colored slaves, not distributed generally over the Union, but localized in the Southern part of it. These slaves constituted a peculiar and powerful interest. All knew that this interest was, somehow, the cause of the war. To strengthen, perpetuate, and extend this interest was the object for which the insurgents would rend the Union, even by war; while the government claimed no right to do more than to restrict the territorial enlargement of it. Neither party expected for the war, the magnitude, or the duration, which it has already attained. Neither anticipated that the <u>cause</u> of the conflict might cease with, or even before, the conflict itself should cease. Each looked for an easier triumph, and a result less fundamental and astounding. Both read the same Bible, and pray to the same God; and each invokes His aid against the other. It may seem strange that any men should dare to ask a just God's assistance in wringing their bread from the sweat of other men's faces; but let us judge not that we be not judged. The prayers of both could not be answered; that of neither has been answered fully. The Almighty has His own purposes. "Woe unto the world because of offences! for it must needs be that offences come; but woe to *that man by whom the offence cometh!" If we shall suppose that American Slavery is one of those offences which, in the providence of God, must needs come, but which, having continued through His appointed time, He now wills to remove, and that He gives to both North and South, this terrible war as the woe due to those by whom the offence came, shall we discern therein any departure from those divine attributes which the believers in a Living God always ascribe to Him? Fondly do we hope—fervently do we pray—that this mighty scourge of war may speedily pass away. Yet, if God wills that it continue, until all the wealth piled by the bond-man's two hundred and fifty years of unrequited toil shall be sunk, and until every drop of blood drawn with the lash, shall be paid by another drawn with the sword, as was said three thousand years ago, so still it must be said "the judgments of the Lord, are true and righteous altogether."*

With malice toward none; with charity for all; with firmness in the right, as God gives us to see the right, let us strive on to finish the work we are in; to bind up the nation's wounds; to care for him who shall have borne the battle, and for his widow, and his orphan—to do all which may achieve and cherish a just, and a lasting peace, among ourselves, and with all nations.

1
Deployment and Discovery

A student of the Civil War is drawn to its battlefields. Gettysburg, Pennsylvania often ranks high on a list of battlefield locations to visit. The magnitude of the struggle and the sacrifices of soldiers from North and South forever altered the history of the town, its fields, and forests during July 1, 2, and 3, 1863. Gettysburg was transformed into a place of valor and sacrifice, honor and reflection, study and awe.

Students of the Gettysburg battle want to learn and understand the movements of men and matériel. They are fascinated by the ebb and flow of the battle, the positions of both armies, the choices of their generals. They become keenly aware of strategic placements and the reasons behind them. They also wonder why some decisions were made regarding formations, attacks, and defense. They look closely at alternatives that only hindsight can offer.

Eager inquirers' desires for knowledge run deep. They study the words and deeds of leaders thoroughly, yearning to know how they intersected. Profound expressions and courageous acts emerging from this battle become topics of diligent and ongoing research.

One of the great collections of words the Gettysburg conflict gave us was the Gettysburg Address. This two-minute speech was presented by Abraham Lincoln on November 19, 1863. The oration was delivered as part of the dedication of a national cemetery built to honor the Union soldiers who had died on that battlefield in July of that year. The speech fulfilled its stated purpose and more. Its message brought a new understanding of the character of the country and encouraged the war-weary nation to stay its course and grapple with its destiny. Its words challenged the people of that day to understand war and peace, conflict and resolution.

One would be hard pressed to plumb the depths of the Gettysburg Address without desiring to learn more about the leader who composed and delivered it. The oration is a classic, of course. For conciseness of thought, brevity of presentation, and endurance of meaning, its aggregation of poignant truths has never been equaled. Abraham Lincoln had created a masterful, enduring communication that touched and inspired all who studied it. It still does.

Lessons of War

The student of history who appreciates the Gettysburg Address is led to cherish many other speeches of this wartime president. Lincoln's Second Inaugural Address is an example. The Second Inaugural stands alongside the Gettysburg Address as one of Lincoln's finest presentations, and for good reason. From these two orations learners and leaders yearn to discover *how* Lincoln processed and expressed information. They endeavor to understand *why* the words delivered in 1863 at Gettysburg and in 1865 at Washington, D.C. moved audiences and continue to influence people now.

Explorers of Civil War battles and utterances uncover resounding and repeating themes in Lincoln's written and spoken offerings—fundamental and enduring principles of leadership—at virtually every turn. The country's faith in itself, its fate as a young nation, and its future as an eternal force for good in the world all were shaped by words and works of a leader who sought to preserve the Union through its most devastating conflict.

Strong leadership principles emerge in a study of this kind. An abiding appreciation of history, a long-term vision for generations yet unborn, bold strategies of winning over an enemy, resolving conflict between former combatants, ultimate sacrifices and requirements of duty, tough decision making, and clear communication are a few of them.

Lasting leadership principles span more than the Civil War, of course. Enduring lessons of leadership live for all time. They outlast conflict because they encompass eternal and uplifting values. These principles when applied empower a warrior to face virtually any challenge with right motives and honorable deeds. Effective leaders rest their choices of action on truths that abide when called upon to make momentous decisions and follow through.

In 2009, the book, *Lincoln, Leadership and Gettysburg* was released. This work discussed the leadership lessons revealed within the Gettysburg Address. It showed that in his speech of only 267 words Lincoln presented the causes and significance of the Gettysburg battle and the Civil War. It documented how he anchored his comments on a key phrase from the Declaration of Independence, declaring again that this nation was *"...dedicated to the proposition that all men are created equal."* The book concluded that his message, theme, and timing were appropriate for his audience in 1863 and that his content and application remain significant for the generations that have come after. (See www.Lincoln-Leadership-Gettysburg.com.)

Lessons of War—Lincoln's Second Inaugural Address, Leadership at Gettysburg builds upon those truths. While both books stand alone, together they create a wider understanding of the leadership lessons contained in the Gettysburg Address and the Second Inaugural Address, as well as the application of those principles during Lincoln's time in office.

The Civil War consumed Lincoln's presidency. After the war opened on April 12, 1861 there was never a time during his two terms in office that fighting was not occurring. When

Lessons of War

Robert E. Lee surrendered to Ulysses S. Grant on April 9, 1865 at Appomattox Court House, Virginia that capitulation guaranteed a Union victory, yet fighting continued elsewhere for weeks. Lincoln was assassinated on April 14, 1865. As Commander-in-Chief he never knew peace—he did not live to see the end of the war he desperately wanted to avoid, yet upon its commencement became firmly dedicated to win.

Lincoln's First Inaugural Address was delivered on March 4, 1861. In this speech the president pleaded for national unity, to avert war, stating succinctly, *"In your hands, my dissatisfied fellow countrymen, and not in mine, is the momentous issue of civil war. The Government will not assail you. You can have no conflict without being yourselves the aggressors. You have no oath registered in heaven to destroy the Government, while I shall have the most solemn one to 'preserve, protect, and defend it.'"* Four years of bloody conflict ensued.

On the occasion of the Second Inaugural Address delivered March 4, 1865 the fighting had not yet ceased, but a fresh hope had arisen that the war would soon end. *"Now, at the expiration of four years, during which public declarations have been constantly called forth on every point and phase of the great contest which still absorbs the attention, and engrosses the energies of the nation, little that is new could be presented. The progress of our arms, upon which all else chiefly depends, is as well known to the public as to myself; and it is, I trust, reasonably satisfactory and encouraging to all. With high hope for the future, no prediction in regard to it is ventured."*

The Second Inaugural Address and the Gettysburg Address

are masterpieces of communication and literature. People who have visited the Lincoln Memorial in Washington, D.C. view both speeches inscribed in stone on the inside walls of the edifice. Both orations were delivered before anyone knew how the Civil War would end and both provided long-term views of attaining positive outcomes for the nation when the war would finally come to a close.

Lessons of War—Lincoln's Second Inaugural Address, Leadership at Gettysburg reveals vital and enduring leadership truths embedded in Lincoln's Second Inaugural Address. It also shows how the leadership principles articulated in 1865 had been graphically demonstrated during and after the Gettysburg battle in 1863. These are eternal principles. They are practiced by anyone who leads, regardless of title, tenure, position, or status. They include how a leader views the causes of war, how a war is waged, how conquering occurs, and how a conflict should be concluded.

Principles of leadership endure because they are true. They are repeatable and therefore should be repeated. When enacted from right motives they produce positive and enduring results regardless of degrees of negativity and controversy, the time required to see results come to fruition, or the immensity of sacrifice involved. Truth wins eventually because it must.

Conflict has been part of the human experience since the dawn of history. War is only one example of its presence. Opposing views and resultant action occur on many levels.

In any conflict sides in opposition strive for what they believe is right. Compromise is possible only when one or both of the antagonists submit to the other. Compromise fails when ideologies remain too far apart, trust between people is absent, parties are immovably entrenched in their beliefs, and a willingness to consider opposing views does not exist. In these conditions the only remaining choice may be war and conquest, conditions where one side is victorious and the other vanquished.

Division

Universal, peaceful coexistence is impossible
Apart from compromise that must of necessity
Uproot fundamentally held beliefs of groups in opposition.

It is, therefore, unachievable minus conflict.
One wins,
Another loses.

If all bow, who leads, who follows?
The ones to whom deference is paid command willful or
     coerced allegiance.
Obedience shuns dissent.

              Division remains.

Conflict, mid enlightened understandings and overtures of
     peace, momentarily restrained, emerges anew in
     altered forms if the basis points of one side are not
     changed.
Conquests pit ideologies, contrary systems, against each
     other.

Protectionism and arrogance thrive within perspectives their
    owners are convinced are true.

God cannot be for and against
Opposing opinions and cross-purposed practices all at the
    same time.
Willing agreements do not exist where one party's win is
    another's loss.
Forced compliance is the mandate and mission of those who
    conquer.

From *Freedom Light—Expressions of Hope and Evidence* © 2009 Glen Aubrey. Used with permission.

The question for leaders is not whether conflict occurs. The question is how they will deal with it when it comes.

Since the close of 1865, a declared civil war has not been a part of the American experiment, though many struggles continue. Uncivil disputes and arguments appear within human relationships whether war is declared or not: at work, home, school, in extended families, societies, and regimes. Escalating conflict is often accompanied by destructive confrontation. If taken to an extreme, all-out war can be the result.

Lincoln earnestly tried not to engage in civil war, but once war was commenced he would accept nothing less than all-out principled victory no matter the costs. His desire for this kind of victory bade him look to God for guidance. Lincoln avowed submission to God's judgments throughout the mighty crucible the country endured. "*On the occasion corresponding to this four years ago, all thoughts were anxiously directed to an impending civil-war. All dreaded it—all sought to avert it. While the inaugural address was being delivered from this place, devoted altogether to <u>saving</u> the Union without war, insurgent agents were in the city seeking to <u>destroy</u> it without war—seeking to dissolve the Union, and divide effects, by negotiation. Both parties deprecated war, but one of them would <u>make</u> war rather than let the nation survive; and the other would <u>accept</u> war rather than let it perish. And the war came… Fondly do we hope—fervently do we pray—that this mighty scourge of war may speedily pass away. Yet, if God wills that it continue, until all the wealth piled by the bond-man's two hundred and fifty years of unrequited toil shall be sunk, and until every drop of blood drawn with the lash, shall be paid by another drawn with the sword, as was said three thousand years ago, so still it must be said 'the judgments of the Lord, are true and righteous altogether.'"*

When faced with conflict, great leaders embrace and employ abiding principles to bring about resolution and restitution. Devoted students of history who become the leaders of their day actively use the lessons that history has proven reliable.

If you've been a leader for any length of time you have already experienced conflict. Understand how great leaders before you handled their difficult situations and apply their practices in yours. Do what they did to produce profitable outcomes.

The leadership truths revealed in Lincoln's Gettysburg Address and Second Inaugural Address helped the country survive its greatest upheaval. In those troubling times enduring principles produced right actions. Chances for positive results increased.

Lincoln once called the United States, *"the last, best hope of earth."* He believed the Union was destined to endure for all time. His leadership demonstrated that belief.

If you are the leader, inquire of yourself: "How strong is my belief? In what ways does my leadership bring about positive results?" Great leaders ask these questions, deploy their answers in their circumstances, and seek to discover improved methods of waging, winning, and ending difficult engagements.

Lincoln's leadership held the country together even through war. In his Second Inaugural Address the president revealed how to conclude war and reconcile combatants. Leaders learn these truths and apply them where similar results are desired.

Perhaps in your leadership you are duty-bound to hold your group together despite immense difficulties now. Lincoln sought peaceful resolution upon the conclusion of one of the greatest conflicts the world had ever known. What kind of peaceful end will you try to create in your situation?

2
History Unites Us—Cause and Effect

<u>Fellow Countrymen</u>

At this second appearing to take the oath of the Presidential office, there is less occasion for an extended address than there was at the first. Then a statement, somewhat in detail, of a course to be pursued, seemed fitting and proper. Now, at the expiration of four years, during which public declarations have been constantly called forth on every point and phase of the great contest which still absorbs the attention, and engrosses the energies of the nation, little that is new could be presented. The progress of our arms, upon which all else chiefly depends, is as well known to the public as to myself; and it is, I trust, reasonably satisfactory and encouraging to all. With high hope for the future, no prediction in regard to it is ventured.

Glen Aubrey

This was indeed a *great contest*. Lincoln's use of the words *absorbs* and *engrosses* are telling. The Civil War was expensive. Numbers detailing loss of lives, expenditures of money, and destruction of property were staggering.

According to *Historical Times Encyclopedia of the Civil War,* Edited by Patricia L. Faust (1991), *Numbers and Losses in the Civil War in America 1861-65* by Thomas L. Livermore (1901), and *Regimental Losses in the American Civil War, 1867-1865* by William F. Fox (1889), referenced and quoted on the websites, http://www.civilwarhome.com/warcosts.htm and http://www.civilwarhome.com:

"The approximately 10,455 military engagements, some devastating to human life and some nearly bloodless, plus naval clashes, accidents, suicides, sicknesses, murders, and executions resulted in total casualties of 1,094,453 during the Civil War. The Federals lost 110,100 killed in action and mortally wounded, and another 224,580 to disease. The Confederates lost approximately 94,000 as a result of battle and another 164,000 to disease. Even if one survived a wound, any projectile that hit bone in either an arm or a leg almost invariably necessitated amputation. The best estimate of Federal army personnel wounded is 275,175; naval personnel wounded, 2,226. Surviving Confederate records indicate 194,026 wounded.

"In dollars and cents, the U.S. government estimated Jan. 1863 that the war was costing $2.5 million daily. A final official estimate in 1879 totaled $6,190,000,000. The Confederacy spent perhaps

Lessons of War

$2,099,808,707. By 1906 another $3.3 billion already had been spent by the U.S. government on Northerners' pensions and other veterans' benefits for former Federal soldiers. Southern states and private philanthropy provided benefits to the Confederate veterans. The amount spent on benefits eventually well exceeded the war's original cost.

"Inflation affected both Northern and Southern assets but hit those of the Confederacy harder. Northern currency fluctuated in value, and at its lowest point $2.59 in Federal paper money equaled $1.00 in gold. The Confederate currency so declined in purchasing power that eventually $60-$70 equaled a gold dollar.

"The physical devastation, almost all of it in the South, was enormous: burned or plundered homes, pillaged countryside, untold losses in crops and farm animals, ruined buildings and bridges, devastated college campuses, and neglected roads all left the South in ruins."

Catastrophic losses attended the town of Gettysburg when the war unfolded there in 1863. These are chronicled in a book I am fortunate to have in my Lincoln Library, *The Three Days at Gettysburg* written by John E. Pitzer, Gettysburg, PA., Member Post 9, G. A. R. (Grand Army of the Republic) and published by *"News" Press, Gettysburg, Pa.* circa 1900. This paperback book of 100 pages is an invaluable resource. Its title page bears the following inscription: "Three Days at Gettysburg, A Complete Hand-Book of the Movements of Both Armies during Lee's Invasion of Pennsylvania, and His Return to Virginia, The

Three Days Battle at Gettysburg, July 1st, 2nd and 3rd, 1863, And a Guide to the Position of each Federal Organization Marked with a Monument or Tablet on the Gettysburg Battlefield, with Casualties of Both Union and Confederate Forces."

The text on the inside front cover shows a slice of contemporary life and economics. The need to advertise then was as important as it is now: "PITZER HOUSE, 143 Main St., known as Chambersburg St., Gettysburg, PA. Boarding and Lodging, Warm and Cold Baths. The Only Temperance House. You will find it Pleasant and Homelike. Give us a Trial. Rates $1.00 to $1.25 Per Day. Teams and Guides, To all Points of Interest on the Battlefield Including a Good Substantial Dinner for $1.25. Satisfaction Guaranteed. JOHN E. PITZER, Member Post 9, G. A. R."

On page 13, Pitzer lists Union casualties from July 1 – 4 as follows: officers killed, 247; enlisted men killed, 2825; officers wounded 1,139 and enlisted men wounded 13,358. Captured or missing: officers 182, enlisted men 5,252, for a total casualty count of 23,003.

Confederate losses are found on Page 78: killed, 2592, wounded, 12,709, and missing, 5,150 for a casualty total of 20,451. For a town numbering approximately 2,500 residents when the battle descended upon it, these numbers graphically illustrate what was noted in *Lincoln, Leadership and Gettysburg* on pages 56 and 57, "The battle brought an additional 165,000 persons, with 72,000 horses, along with winding and lengthy columns of war materiel, including ammunition caissons and wagons carrying mountains of supplies in support of two huge armies. This invasion of people and provisions bloated the town, straining its meager resources."

Photographs taken at the time illustrate these statistics. Poignant images of devastation at Gettysburg became permanently lodged into the nation's conscience as it weighed and paid the price of war.

Great leaders recognize the value of understanding current conditions, their causes, costs, and effects. Leaders work to improve the negative circumstances that confront them. Leaders do not dwell in vacuums of information when called upon to right wrongful conditions. On the contrary, leaders learn and get involved.

Shared history unites all those who live and labor through it. It also unites those who come after who want to learn its facts and impacts. One of the great challenges for any leader working within negative circumstances is to recognize the need for change and take the initiative to make it happen. This is the work of winning.

Such was the situation faced by the 20th Maine Regiment under the leadership of Colonel Joshua Chamberlain on July 2, 1863 at Gettysburg. Chamberlain and his regiment had been placed just beneath the crest of Little Round Top, a point that made up the far left flank of the Union line. Chamberlain had received an order from Colonel Strong Vincent to "hold at all costs."

The reason for the directive was simple enough. Leaders from both armies recognized the strategic value of the location. They knew that if the Union defenders were overrun the flank would be compromised and the entire Union line threatened.

Chamberlain took his charge seriously and acted courageously. Southern attacks upon his position from the Fifteenth and Forty-seventh Alabama continued relentlessly. Soon a lack of ammunition became a serious problem for the boys in blue. Combined with mounting casualties, the decision to hold the flank meant that something extraordinary had to be done.

The events that followed showcased how leadership confronted and changed formidable and foreboding circumstances despite mounting loss. The principle is this: leaders consider their conditions and act decisively to create better results for the long term, though faced with the daunting crucible of sacrifice in the short term.

In *The Three Days at Gettysburg* Pitzer noted the losses of the Gettysburg engagements for the 20th Maine, page 66: the 20th Maine numbered 358 at the start and lost 132. On page 81 he detailed that Law's Brigade commanded by Brig. Gen. E. McIver Law brought into action 1,500 men and lost 550. Of these Col. William C. Oates, 15th Alabama, lost 83 and the 47th Alabama commanded by Col. James L. Sheffield, Lieut. Col. M. J. Bulger, and Maj. J. M. Campbell lost 40.

John Heiser, Historian, National Park Service, Gettysburg National Military Park, provided updated and more accurate information: "Pitzer's numbers are only for those captured in the 15th Alabama. According to more reliable research in John Busey's book, *Regimental Strengths and Losses at Gettysburg* (Longstreet House, Hightstown, NJ, 1982), Law's brigade numbered 1,933 with 535 total casualties. The 15th Alabama Infantry lost 178 killed, wounded and missing out of 499. The 47th Alabama lost 69 out of 347."

In 1913 General Joshua Chamberlain himself wrote an account of his experiences with the 20th Maine Regiment on Little Round Top, published in *Hearst's Magazine* and reprinted by Stan Clark Military Books of Gettysburg, Pennsylvania, Copyright 1994. This quote from pages 22 and 23 is used with permission:

"Not a moment was about to be lost! Five minutes more of such a defensive, and the last roll-call would sound for us! Desperate as the chances were, there was nothing for it, but to take the offensive. I stepped to the colors. The men turned towards me. One word was enough,—'BAYONETS!'—It caught like fire, and swept along the ranks. The men took it up with a shout, one could not say, whether from the pit, or the song of the morning star! It was vain to order 'Forward.' No mortal could have heard it in the mighty hosanna that was winging the sky. Nor would he wait to hear. There are things still as of the first creation, "whose seed is in itself." The grating clash of steel in fixing bayonets told its own story; the color rose in front; the whole line quivered for the start; the edge of the left-wing rippled, swung, tossed among the rocks, straightened, changed curve from scimitar to sickle-shape; and the bristling archers swooped down upon the serried host—down into the face of half a thousand! Two hundred men!"

Whether the bayonet charge was ordered by Chamberlain or it occurred by forced exigencies of circumstance, it happened and it worked. Taking the initiative immediately changed the consequences and helped win that battle for the Union.

Chamberlain worked within his assignment. Seeing the need, he produced new actions designed to alter negative circumstances and he accomplished a strategic victory.

Leaders do this. In any conflict where a superior goal is declared, firm decisions are made and actions are committed toward their fulfillment. In this the leader sets the pace. Great leaders refuse to endlessly tolerate demoralizing conditions where a higher cause demands fresh actions to achieve improved results. Great leaders act and do so with confidence.

History unites us. Wittingly or not, all share its effects. While factors may differ, principles of cause and effect remain fixed.

Students of history observe its incidents and issues. They learn from the mistakes and successes of the past. Leaders of today embrace and activate the lessons that have been shown to endure. One of them is this: if a condition is to be improved, leaders act decisively when causes and choices are shown to be right.

Great leaders take the initiative. They change their

circumstances for the better. They work diligently to produce positive results for themselves and those they lead. They know that the good they accomplish will forever affect the outcome of a conflict and those who live beyond it.

3
Conflict Comes

On the occasion corresponding to this four years ago, all thoughts were anxiously directed to an impending civil-war. All dreaded it—all sought to avert it. While the inaugural address was being delivered from this place, devoted altogether to <u>saving</u> the Union without war, insurgent agents were in the city seeking to <u>destroy</u> it without war—seeking to dissolve the Union, and divide effects, by negotiation. Both parties deprecated war, but one of them would <u>make</u> war rather than let the nation survive; and the other would <u>accept</u> war rather than let it perish. And the war came.

One eighth of the whole population were colored slaves, not distributed generally over the Union, but localized in the Southern part of it. These slaves constituted a peculiar and powerful interest. All knew that this interest was, somehow, the cause of the war. To strengthen, perpetuate, and extend this interest was the object for which the insurgents would rend the Union, even by war; while the government claimed no right to do more than to restrict the territorial enlargement of it.

Great leaders strive for peace. They look for points of agreement upon which resolution can be built and order maintained. They understand that conflict is costly and desire to avoid it. They also recognize that sometimes bold confrontation cannot be prevented. When ideology demands that a contest must decide which precepts and practices shall stand, the leader does not shrink from the responsibility the contest presents.

While conflict is seen in international war it also emerges in other more localized arenas. From *Core Teams Work Their Principles and Practices* by Glen Aubrey, Copyright 2007: "Expect conflict to be a part of the human experience. Seen in work, family, social settings, or any environment where people interact, conflict is probable where more than one person is present."

This truth is evidenced in business group interactions. "Because participants on a core team are not robots, they will sometimes oppose each other relationally or functionally. In fact, some of the greatest solution provision may originate from challenging interchanges. Handle them well. Conflict that divides, casts negative aspersions, builds barricades to communication, and destroys healthy relationships is generally discord that is not being dealt with appropriately or in a timely manner. If a team wants to continue to grow through trying experiences, it will find and utilize proven methods to resolve conflicts, and mature each other through the process."

In any environment opposing ideologies seek to advance their beliefs. This is natural. When two or more sides' opinions are at odds, and compromise is not optional or exercised, conflict can emerge.

An organization faced with opposition studies its disagreements and carefully weighs whether conflict should be conducted. Effective leadership views the whole picture before deciding which pieces, if any, should be addressed. A leader considers the importance of impending confrontation to see if the costs of the contest and its resolution merit the fight.

Where the decision is made that conflict is the only way resolution can occur, the wise leader matches the degree of confrontation with the resources at hand and selects appropriate methods to bring resolution and eventual cessation of argument. A strong leader defines the engagement, designs its means, and chooses the best ways to conduct and conclude it.

Lincoln understood the efforts "insurgent agents" were making to avert civil war. He was fully aware of the ongoing negotiations that sought peace at the price of dissolution of the Union. In eloquent lines the president summed up the convictions, actions, and results of these contestants: "*Both parties deprecated war, but one of them would make war rather than let the nation survive; and the other would accept war rather than let it perish. And the war came.*"

Consider the principles in opposition. At the very least, the South was dedicated to States' rights, including protecting and expanding the institution of slavery. The North was committed to the preservation of the Union and "restricting the territorial enlargement" of slavery. These two positions could not be reconciled. They escalated to the point of dissolution. By the time of Lincoln's first inauguration seven states had already seceded from the Union: South Carolina, Mississippi, Florida, Alabama, Georgia, Louisiana, and Texas.

Lincoln used the phrase *a peculiar and powerful interest* to describe slavery as a cause of the Civil War. Note that the president did not use this speech as an opportunity to disclose fully all the reasons for the war; rather, he stated, *"All knew that this interest was, somehow, the cause of the war."*

There is an important leadership truth here: though it may not be possible to know *all* the reasons behind a conflict, certain causes are *somehow* understood. Debates and arguments can rage unceasingly, finding fault and fixing blame. Endless discussions can become exercises in futility in efforts to fully comprehend full motive and origin. Leadership recognizes that a point can be reached where mere words can never describe the full extent of *why*, though the conflict is present and must be dealt with. Great leaders choose to accept what they may not know while endeavoring mightily to uphold a greater cause and deal effectively with what they do know.

Countless discourses and debates defined and reinforced

the positions of the opposing parties in Lincoln's day. Words morphed into war when the divisions between their positions became too great to bridge. Early in the morning of April 12, 1861 the first shots were fired at Fort Sumter in the Charleston Harbor and the Civil War began.

Conflict can develop regardless of the desires and efforts to avoid it. Events at Gettysburg in 1863 poignantly illustrate this. The town had become a strategic location for both armies. It was a hub for ten roads that intersected within its limits. Citizens by and large did not comprehend the importance of their place to the war efforts, at least at first. They concluded that the war simply came upon them—they certainly had not planned to host it.

Civilian accounts of the battle on July 1, 2, and 3 are of great interest. One is particularly captivating. The book, *At Gettysburg or What a Girl Saw and Heard of the Battle—A True Narrative* was written by Mrs. Tillie (Pierce) Alleman twenty-five years after the battle. She was about fifteen years of age when the Gettysburg battle occurred. Her book was published privately in 1888. New material was copyrighted in 1987 and the book was reprinted and distributed by Butternut and Blue, and Stan Clark Military Books, in 1994. The following passages from pages 15 and 16 are quoted with permission.

These observations are those of a hometown girl who saw events unfold firsthand. "My native townsmen, during that terrible struggle, acted as patriotic and bravely as it was possible for citizens to act, who had suddenly thrust upon them the most gigantic battle of modern times.

"They had none of the weapons or munitions of war; they were not drilled and were totally unprepared for such an unthoughtof [sic] experience, They were civilians."

They rose to the occasion. "Upon the first rumor of the rebel invasion, Major Robert Bell, a citizen of the place, recruited a company of cavalry from the town and surrounding country.

"A company of infantry was also formed from the students and citizens of the place which was mustered into Col. Wm. Jennings' regiment and Pennsylvania Emergency Troops.

"This regiment, on June 26th, was the first to encounter and exchange shots with the invaders of 1863. Though inexperienced, the stand they made, and the valor they displayed before an overwhelming force, cannot fail in placing the loyalty and bravery of her citizens in foremost rank."

Conflict usually affects a greater number of people than those who conduct it. Leaders know this. They seek to minimize collateral damage though sometimes their efforts fail. From *Lincoln, Leadership and Gettysburg*, page 56: "Gettysburg comprises an immense battlefield. The vastness of the landscape reminds one of the larger panoramas of our lives, where struggles ensue and losses and gains compose the experiences of life. The Gettysburg National Military Park covers more than 6,000 acres alone. The sites of the three-day conflict consumed the town and surrounding areas in 1863, and they still do today."

People touched by conflict, no matter its origin, are changed.

Whether combatants or bystanders their experiences become a part of them for the rest of their lives. Effects last a very long time. While some may seek to dismiss them casually or quickly, all make their mark.

Memories of conflict regardless of scope are often accompanied by pain. This pain may be exceedingly difficult to deal with or impossible to completely erase. Perhaps eradicating pain shouldn't be the goal anyway, but learning how to deal with it certainly is. Scars from negative encounters usually remain—they rarely go away on their own. They're not designed to.

A story from the Bible illustrates this. Most have heard the account of "Doubting Thomas." This moniker is used to describe individuals who are not convinced with the truth of a matter until they experience it for themselves.

The incident of Doubting Thomas is recorded in the Gospel of John, Chapter 20:19-29. It goes like this: after the resurrection of Christ, the disciples were gathered together in secret, though Thomas, one of the disciples, was absent. The passage declares that Christ appeared to the group and that they were amazed to see Him and glad at His presence. Following the encounter the disciples related the event to Thomas. Thomas doubted them and told them he would not believe unless he placed his finger into the nail scars of Jesus' hands and put his hand into the place on Jesus' side where a Roman spear had been thrust on the day of His crucifixion.

The account goes on to say that eight days later the disciples were gathered again but this time Thomas was present. Jesus appeared to them and invited Thomas to do exactly what Thomas had said he wanted to do. The story states that Thomas believed because of that encounter though we are not told if Thomas ever placed his finger and hand into the wounds' locations.

The point here is this: in the account, though Jesus had experienced a resurrection, had been transformed, and was able to appear and disappear, *the scars from the crucible of His cross remained.*

Whether caused by participation in conflict or observance of its destruction, pain exists. It can be worked through, dreadful memories dealt with, forgiveness freely offered and received, appalling losses assuaged, and processes of grieving completed. Healing should include these efforts and effects.

But scars remain. These enduring marks represent more than memory; they reveal sacrifice, suffering, service, and standing up for belief. They remind their bearer of wounds and sorrow, healing and resolve. Scars instruct in arenas that only hurts can know.

In the final analysis, these disfigured marks compose a part of life's legacy of fuller understanding. They should be embraced. Their remembrances bear residual effects of controversy, conflict, conquest, or being conquered. They teach valuable life lessons to those who care enough to embrace their presence and meaning. Don't hide them; they are there to help you and the people you touch.

Lessons of War

A Choice Away

Nearly removed,
Viewed from afar ere longing dies,
Desire churns from secreted innermost regions,
    seeking to be replenished.

Nourished, a pilgrim recognizes distraught yet familiar voices
Piercing love's lost and latent, distanced voids
Where destinies abide subjected to their owners.

Cloistered, moved upon the board,
Represented, yet unreachable,
Restless hearts seek reasons and reach for the unattainable.

Choices beam a dream's pursuit in graceful diligence
Where remains the perfect plan,
Though oft its stains and scars are permanent.

From *Freedom Light—Expressions of Hope and Evidence* © 2009 Glen Aubrey. Used with permission.

Effective leaders understand that the results of conflicts, regardless of size, can generate recurring negative repercussions if not dealt with appropriately. They also learn how valuable the effects of conflicts can be. The methods used to deal with conflict, including its pain and scars, indicate health or disease, victory or victimization.

Conflict comes. Its causes vary. Some are known, others not. Learn this lesson if you are the leader: when conflict comes, no matter its source, perform your role to affect its course.

4

The Unexpected Price of Winning

Neither party expected for the war, the magnitude, or the duration, which it has already attained. Neither anticipated that the <u>cause</u> of the conflict might cease with, or even before, the conflict itself should cease. Each looked for an easier triumph, and a result less fundamental and astounding.

Soldiers of the North and South fought for diverse reasons. Some wanted to experience the thrill of battle, while others sought to defend principles and practices they believed were right. Regardless of their motives, at the outset few thought the war would last beyond several skirmishes or one or two larger scale battles. Some were convinced that the Battle of Bull Run (or Manassas Junction) during July of 1861 would decide the whole thing. It didn't.

On April 15, 1861 President Lincoln issued a proclamation calling for 75,000 militiamen to fight for the Union. The language of this proclamation is revealing.

BY THE PRESIDENT OF THE UNITED STATES: A PROCLAMATION

Whereas the laws of the United States have been for some time past and now are opposed and the execution thereof obstructed in the States of South Carolina, Georgia, Alabama, Florida, Mississippi, Louisiana, and Texas by combinations too powerful to be suppressed by the ordinary course of judicial proceedings or by the powers vested in the marshals by law:

Now, therefore, I, Abraham Lincoln, President of the United States in virtue of the power in me vested by the Constitution and the laws, have thought fit to call forth, and hereby do call forth, the militia of the several States of the Union, to the aggregate number of 75,000, in order to suppress said combinations and to cause the laws to be duly executed.

The details of this object will be immediately communicated to the State authorities through the War Department.

I appeal to all loyal citizens to favor, facilitate, and aid this effort to maintain the honor, the integrity, and the existence of our National Union, and the perpetuity of popular government, and to redress wrongs already long enough endured.

I deem it proper to say that the first service assigned to the forces hereby called forth will probably be to repossess the forts, places, and property which have been seized from the Union, and in every event the utmost care will be observed, consistently with the objects aforesaid, to avoid any devastation, any destruction of or interference with property, or any disturbance of peaceful citizens in any part of the country.

And I hereby command the persons composing the combinations aforesaid to disperse and retire peaceably to their respective abodes within twenty days from date.

Deeming that the present condition of public affairs presents an extraordinary occasion, I do hereby, in virtue of the power in me vested by the Constitution, convene both houses of Congress.

Senators and Representatives are therefore summoned to assemble at their respective chambers at twelve o'clock noon on Thursday, the fourth day of July next, then and there to consider and determine such measures as in their wisdom the public safety and interest may seem to demand.

In witness whereof I have hereunto set my hand and caused the seal of the United States to be affixed.

Done at the city of Washington this fifteenth day of April, in the year of our Lord one thousand eight hundred and sixty-one, and of the Independence of the United States the eighty-fifth.

ABRAHAM LINCOLN

Lincoln correctly observed that his purpose as president was to uphold the laws of the land. The seven states that had already seceded had opposed and obstructed the laws, "*...by combinations too powerful to be suppressed by the ordinary course of judicial proceedings or by the powers vested in the marshals by law.*" Dramatic and effective action was called for. Lincoln responded.

Time would reveal that following the initial call to military service the war would rapidly escalate. By the time it concluded, over 600,000 combatants on both sides would have died of wounds and disease. Over three days and in the weeks that followed, the Gettysburg battle alone would produce a casualty count in excess of 50,000.

To use Lincoln's phrase from the Second Inaugural, *"neither party"* expected the awful results they had witnessed and experienced since the first 75,000 soldiers were summoned. Winning was to come at an unexpected price for both sides.

In any argument that escalates to blows the costs of the engagement cannot be determined fully when the conflict begins. No one at Gettysburg knew the price they would pay.

Near the intersection of Reynolds Avenue and the Chambersburg Pike (Route U.S. 30) stands a monument dedicated in 1889. It honors the 143rd Pennsylvania Regiment and the heroic sacrifice of Color Sergeant Ben Crippen. On the first day of battle, July 1, 1863, this regiment, though severely outnumbered, fought bravely to ward off a strong Confederate advance.

The Historical Record, Press of the Wilkes-Barre Record, 1888, in an article titled, "The Monument of the 143d." relates this story beginning on page 107: "In the course of his oration at the dedication of the 143d monument at Gettysburg on last week, Gen. E. S. Osborne, of this city, referred feelingly to Gen. E. L. Dana, who as colonel commanded the regiment July 1, 1863. Gen. Osborne told of the wonderful heroism of the regiment—how they changed front under fire and held their position five hours. Speaking of the brave action of brave Crippen, he said: 'There are many instances of exceeding valor and personal individual heroism—but no better ever occurred anywhere than right here and by this regiment. The order had been given to fall back. One man did not hear it. That man was Ben Crippen, the color sergeant. He faced the enemy. He had not heard the order to fall back. The rebels were coming on, and yet with a defiant air and clenched fist he stood there. It is [sic] happened that major Conyngham saw Ben Crippen defying the whole rebel army. Promptly he cried out, "Rally, 143d, rally on your colors." Capt. DeLacy, the man who never goes to sleep and is always where he should be, also saw Crippen. He caught up the cry and his voice called out, "Rally, 143d, on your colors." Then along the whole line went the startling command, "Rally, 143d, on your colors." Did the regiment keep falling back? Not a bit of it. With Conyngham, DeLacy, Crippen and Blair in the line they did rally on the colors, and took them safely from the field. But poor Ben Crippen didn't go with them. He laid his life down on this field and the 143d carried the colors away, and they remained with the regiment to inspire it with courage and glory on other fields.'"

According to several accounts Sgt. Crippen was nearly 6' 1" tall. His height, as well as his standard, made him an easy target. His body was never found and it is presumed that Crippen is one of the soldiers buried in the National Cemetery, designated "unknown."

At another Gettysburg battlefield location, Cemetery Ridge,

visitors learn of the costly sacrifice of the 1st Minnesota Infantry Regiment, commanded by Colonel William Colvill. The story is told in an article titled, "The First Minnesota at Gettysburg. By Lieutenant William Lochren, First Minnesota Infantry, U. S. Volunteers., Read January 14, 1890." published in *Glimpses of the Nation's Struggle., Third Series., Papers Read Before The Minnesota Commandery of the Military Order of The Loyal Legion of the United States, 1889 – 1892*, Published for the Commandery, Chaplain Edward D. Neill, D.D., Editor., D. D. Merrill Company, New York., St. Paul., Minneapolis., 1893., Copyright, 1893, D. D. Merrill Company.

The account begins on page 47. "Soon after noon Sickles advanced the line of the Third Corps more than half a mile, to a slight ridge near the Emmettsburg [sic] road, his left reaching the Devil's Den, near the base of Little Round Top; and the remaining eight companies of the First Minnesota, reduced by the casualties of war to two hundred and sixty-two men, were sent to the centre [sic] of the position just vacated by Sickles's [sic] advance, to support Battery C of the Fourth U. S. Artillery. No other troops were near us, and we stood in full view of Sickles's battle in the Peach Orchard, and witnessed with eager anxiety the varying fortunes of that sanguinary conflict, until at length, with gravest apprehension, we saw our men give way before the heavier forces of Longstreet and Hill, and come back, slowly at first and rallying at short intervals, but soon broken and in utter disorder, rushing down the slope, by the Trostle House, across the low ground, up the slope on our side, and past our position to the rear, followed by a heavy force of the Confederates, the large brigades of Wilcox and Barksdale, in regular lines, coming steadily on in the flush of victory, and firing on the fugitives. They reached the low ground, and in a few minutes would be at our position on the rear of the left flank of our army, which they could roll up as Jackson did the Eleventh Corps at Chancellorsville. There was no organized force to oppose them but our handful of two hundred and sixty-two men.

"Most soldiers, in the face of the near advance of such an overpowering force, which had just defeated the bulk of an army corps, would have caught the panic and joined the retreating forces. But the First Minnesota had never deserted any post, had never retired without orders; and, desperate as the situation seemed, and as it was, the regiment stood firm against whatever might come. Just then (General Winfield Scott) Hancock, with a single aide, rode up at full speed, and for a moment vainly endeavored to rally Sickles's retreating forces. Reserves had been sent for, but were too far away to hope to reach the critical position until it should be occupied by the enemy, unless that enemy were stopped. Quickly leaving the fugitives, Hancock spurred to where we stood, calling out as he reached us, 'What regiment is this?' 'First Minnesota,' replied Colvill. 'Charge those lines!' commanded Hancock. Every man realized in an instant what that order meant—death or wounds to us all, the sacrifice of the regiment to gain a few minutes' time and save the position. And every man saw and accepted the necessity for the sacrifice; and in a moment, responding to Colvill's rapid orders, the regiment, in perfect line, with arms at 'right shoulder, shift,' was sweeping down the slope directly upon the enemy's centre. No hesitation, no stopping to fire, though the men fell fast at every stride before the concentrated fire of the whole Confederate force, directed upon us as soon as the movement was observed. Silently, without orders, and almost from the start, 'double-quick' had changed to utmost speed, for in utmost speed lay the only hope that any of us could pass through that storm of lead and strike the enemy. 'Charge!' shouted Colvill as we neared the first line, and with leveled bayonets, at full speed, we rushed upon it, fortunately, as it was slightly disordered in crossing a dry brook. The men were never made who will stand against leveled bayonets coming with such momentum and evident desperation. The first line broke in our front as we reached it, and rushed back through the second line, stopping the whole advance. We then poured in our first fire, and availing ourselves of such shelter as the low bank of the dry brook afforded, held the entire force at bay for a considerable time, and until our reserves appeared on the ridge we had left. Had the enemy rallied quickly to a countercharge, its overwhelming numbers would have crushed us in a moment, and we would have effected but a slight pause in its advance. But the ferocity of our onset seemed to paralyze them for a time, and though they poured in a terrible and continuous fire from the front and enveloping flanks, they kept at a respectful distance from our bayonets, until, before the added fire of our fresh reserves, they began to retire and we were ordered back.

"What Hancock had given us to do was done thoroughly. The regiment had stopped the enemy, held back its mighty force, and saved the position, and probably that battle-field [sic]. But at what a sacrifice! Nearly every officer was dead, or lay weltering with bloody wounds—our gallant colonel and every field-officer among them. Of the two hundred and sixty-two men who made the charge, two hundred and fifteen lay upon the field, struck down by Rebel bullets; forty-seven men were still in line, and not a man missing. The annals of war contain no parallel to this charge. In its desperate valor, complete execution, successful result, and in its sacrifice of men in proportion to the number engaged, authentic history has not record with which it can be compared."

If that sacrifice from this regiment wasn't enough, the survivors of this action on July 2nd also helped repulse Pickett's Charge on July 3rd. Also called Longstreet's Assault, this charge is another graphic illustration of immense and awful sacrifice. The movement involved from 12,000 - 15,000 men. After a massive cannonade from over one hundred Confederate guns firing toward the Union lines, the Confederates marched east across the open fields between Seminary Ridge and Cemetery Ridge. The expanse they had to cover under heavy fire extended for more than a mile.

It may be hard to imagine what drove these men to advance

in such exposed positions. Thousands were killed. Thousands more were wounded.

General George Pickett, for whom the charge is usually named, lost over half of his division, nearly 3,000 men. Of his fifteen regimental commanders, six were mortally wounded or killed. The others were wounded with only one surviving unscathed. A famous account exists of a conversation that occurred when Pickett returned to the Confederate lines. General Robert E. Lee ordered Pickett to prepare his division for a possible Union counterattack. Pickett is said to have replied, "General Lee, I have no division now."

Over the course of the Civil War an "easier triumph" became a distant and unrealized dream and "...*a result less fundamental and astounding*" was not to be seen. Armies grew larger. Increasing amounts of munitions of war were employed. Sacrifices mounted. Staggering numbers of lives were lost.

Here is the lesson for leaders: weigh carefully the costs of war, including the trials of conflict and responsibilities of victory. In nearly every case the price of winning will exceed its original estimate.

5
Belief and Practice—Faith Tried and Tested

Both read the same Bible, and pray to the same God; and each invokes His aid against the other. It may seem strange that any men should dare to ask a just God's assistance in wringing their bread from the sweat of other men's faces; but let us judge not that we be not judged. The prayers of both could not be answered; that of neither has been answered fully.

Lincoln was a man of faith though he was not "religious" as some would define the term. There is no doubt that he believed in God. That belief was demonstrated in Lincoln's dependence upon Higher Authority, and seemed to grow over time. There is also no doubt he possessed a high degree of intelligence. This president's intellect made him highly analytical. In his Second Inaugural Address Lincoln combined his strong belief and reliance upon God with his exacting logic and keen powers of reasoning and created a masterpiece of faith and fact.

Without a doubt he was in submission to God. From *Lincoln, Leadership and Gettysburg,* pages 95 and 96: "This president admitted he did not understand God's designs fully. Who does? However, Lincoln knew he was part of them…

"During September of 1862 Lincoln wrote his 'Meditation on the Divine Will.' *'The will of God prevails. In great contests each party claims to act in accordance with the will of God. Both may be, and one must be, wrong.'*

"In a letter to Albert Hodges dated April 4, 1864, Lincoln stated, *'If God now wills the removal of a great wrong, and wills also that we of the North as well as you of the South, shall pay fairly for our complicity in that wrong, impartial history will find therein new cause to attest and revere the justice and goodness of God.'*

"Later that same year, in a letter dated September 4 and addressed to Eliza Gurney, he wrote, *'We hoped for a happy termination of this terrible war long before this; but God knows best, and has ruled otherwise. We shall yet acknowledge His wisdom and our own error therein.'"*

In the lines of Second Inaugural quoted above, Lincoln deftly brought out the discrepancy of anyone trying to employ God's aid against an enemy when both sides beseeched the same

God. *"The prayers of both could not be answered; that of neither has been answered fully."*

While admonishing his listeners, *"let us judge not"* Lincoln pointedly classified petitions that asked for God's help for a cause that embraced slavery as "strange." They were strange, and it was right that the president revealed the folly of these requests for divine assistance in support of that dreadful institution.

Judgment was intimated in this case anyway. Without naming the source, he quoted a passage found in Matthew 7:1, a part of the Sermon on the Mount. Lincoln knew his Bible. He read it and referenced it often.

The translation of the Bible Lincoln used was *The King James Version*. It was authorized by King James I of England in 1604. The work was completed in 1611. The use of this version of the Bible was widespread by the nineteenth century and its vocabulary was familiar to most.

Clarence E. Macartney, in *Lincoln and the Bible* (1949), relates a story of an event that occurred in May of 1864. According to the account Lincoln learned that only 400 people had attended a convention in Ohio nominating John C. Frémont for President. "Lincoln took his Bible up from his desk and after a little search came upon the passage which told of David and the company which gathered about him at the cave of Adullam when he was pursued and persecuted by King Saul: 'And everyone that was in distress, and everyone that was in debt, and everyone that was discontented, gathered themselves unto him; and he became a captain over them; and there were with him about four hundred men.'" The passage Lincoln searched for and found was I Samuel 22:2.

Lincoln's knowledge, use, and understanding of scripture permeate his Second Inaugural Address. Deep faith, righteous piety, earnest prayer, and familiarity with the Bible were popular traits during his day. Lincoln combined his common roots, skilled mastery of language, impeccable logic, and deep acquaintance with scripture to communicate with his audience effectively.

In the lines quoted above Lincoln inferred that no one had the right to dare to ask God to do an act that promoted slavery. *"It may seem strange that any men should dare to ask a just God's assistance in wringing their bread from the sweat of other men's faces..."* The implication was that a person who approached God with any intent to enslave and punish another had better be unalterably convinced that he was justified in doing so and not incorrect in his own behavior toward his fellowman. *"...wringing their bread from the sweat of other men's faces"* is strong language. In this expression Lincoln's deep disgust for slavery was boldly revealed as was his strong belief that the people who wanted to perpetuate the institution were promoting and prolonging a grave injustice.

Lincoln had disliked slavery for a long time. In 1837, at age 28, he was a member of the State Legislature in Illinois. On March 3rd of that year Lincoln and fellow Whig, Daniel (Dan) Stone, both Representatives from Sangamon County, issued a protest statement for the record. This statement represented the first public declaration of Lincoln's and Stone's opposition to the institution of slavery.

In part the statement read, "They believe that the institution of slavery is founded on both injustice and bad policy; but that the promulgation of abolition doctrines tends rather to increase than to abate its evils. They believe that the Congress of the United States has no power, under the constitution, to interfere with the institution of slavery in the different States. They believe that the Congress of the United States has the power, under the constitution, to abolish slavery in the District of Columbia; but that that power ought not to be exercised unless at the request of the people of said District…"

Later as President, Lincoln wrote to Horace Greely, Editor of the *New York Tribune*. The date was August 22, 1862. Lincoln was responding to an open letter published by Greely on the 19th in which Greely had intimated that the administration was blundering, without purpose on the war.

In his reply Lincoln articulated his official policy clearly: "*I would save the Union.*" He also said this: "*What I do about slavery, and the colored race, I do because I believe it helps to save the Union; and what I forbear, I forbear because I do not believe it would help to save the Union.*" His purpose was clear. But he wanted his personal preference to be just as clear. He closed his letter to Greely with these words, "*I have here stated my purpose according to my view of official duty; and I intend no modification of my oft-expressed personal wish that all men everywhere could be free.*"

The Civil War forced many who professed Christianity and practiced pious religion to examine their beliefs and weigh how their convictions translated into action. Their very foundations of faith were tried and tested in consideration of questions of loyalty to the Union or Confederacy, and support or lack of it regarding slavery. As Lincoln pointed out, it was incongruent to believe that God could support both sides of a conflict in direct opposition to each other. It was also unreasonable to conclude that God would honor both sides equally as they wantonly tried to kill each other.

One story goes that Lincoln was once asked if God was on the side of the Union. Quoted from http://www.1-famous-quotes.com/quote/6352, Lincoln is said to have responded, "Sir, my concern is not whether God is on our side. My greatest concern is to be on God's side, for God is always right."

While most believed God was always right, many practiced wrong under His banner. Much blood of Christian men on both sides was spilt as many proclaimed the righteousness of their cause.

Christ Lutheran Church is located at #44 Chambersburg Street in Gettysburg, close to the center of town. During the battle of Gettysburg it was known as College Lutheran Church and it served as a hospital. The scenes inside and outside were gruesome on July 1st as over 100 wounded men were laid out in the main sanctuary. Beds were improvised by placing wood boards across the tops of pews. One civilian account recalled,

"Limbs were being amputated and thrown out of the church windows, piling upon the ground below."

On this day the Union First Corps was in full retreat through the town, heading for the protection of Cemetery Hill and Cemetery Ridge. Confederate forces pursued the retreating Union forces, passing in front of the church. The Chaplain of the 90th PA, Reverend Horatio Howell was working alongside medical staff inside the church. Hearing the commotion of the retreat and pursuit, Chaplain Howell decided to step through the front doors of the church and observe what was going on.

The story at http://www.gettysburg.stonesentinels.com/Individuals/Howell.php, recounts it this way: "According to the most likely story, Reverend Howell, wearing a Union officer's uniform complete with sword, was ordered to surrender his weapon by a passing Confederate. Howell tried to explain that he was a noncombatant and did not need to give up his weapon but the Confederate, in the midst of an afternoon of intense fighting, was in no mood to argue."

In a famous narrative written later by Sgt. Archibald Snow and recorded at this website, http://www.chaplainsmuseum.org/i/?p=558, Sgt. Snow related how he followed Howell out of the church. Snow described what occurred. "I had just had my wound dressed and was leaving through the front door just behind Chaplain Howell, at the same time when the advance skirmishers of the Confederates were coming up the street on a run. Howell, in addition to his shoulder straps & uniform, wore the straight dress sword prescribed in Army Regulations for chaplains… The first skirmisher arrived at the food of the church steps as the chaplain and I came out. Placing one foot on the first step the soldier called on the chaplain to surrender; but Howell, instead of throwing up his hands promptly and uttering the usual 'I surrender,' attempted some dignified explanation to the effect that he was a noncombatant and as such was exempt from capture, when a shot from the skirmisher's rifle ended the controversy… The man who fired the shot stood on the exact spot where a memorial tablet has since been erected, and Chaplain Howell, fell upon the landing at the top of the steps."

In 1889 a monument in the form of an open book was placed at the bottom of the church steps. It's still there and reads as follows:

Left Page:

IN MEMORIUM.

REV. HORATIO S. HOWELL

CHAPLAIN.
90th PENN'A VOLS,
WAS CRUELLY SHOT
DEAD ON THESE
CHURCH STEPS ON
THE AFTERNOON OF
JULY 1ST 1863.

Right Page:

"HE DELIVERETH ME
FROM MINE ENEMIES;
YEA, THOU LIFTEST ME
UP ABOVE THOSE THAT
RISE UP AGAINSE ME."
18TH PSALMS
48TH VERSE.
"HE BEING DEAD, YET
SPEAKETH"
HEBREWS 11, 4.TH

An inscription at the bottom of the Howell marker reads:

OUR TRIBUTE
SURVIVORS ASSOCIATION
OF THE 90TH PENN'A VOL'S
AND PERSONAL FRIENDS OF
THE LAMENTED CHAPLAIN

Faith systems in opposition were sorely examined by the circumstances they confronted. Justification of any was difficult if not impossible because full understanding did not and could not exist. Both sides endured sacrifice and suffering and both sides inflicted them upon the other. For some it was "all in the name of God." Defense of one's faith position was, in many cases, subject to the dictates of an army's purpose, however. Seldom were these issues resolved. Perhaps for many they were not understood to any appreciable degree to begin with. Lincoln's words in this piece of the Second Inaugural sought to bring clarity to a confused state where little clarity existed.

Leaders should learn this lesson: combatants may seek to manufacture higher reasons to justify their actions. But beware justifying any activity from a position of ignorance. Higher principles may be at stake. Know them before an action commences and apply them because they're true.

According to Lincoln and his use of the quote from Jesus' Sermon on the Mount, the responsibility was not to judge. Rather, the leader's job was to proclaim principles of truth and to hold unreservedly to them even though complete understanding of what they meant and how they worked might not be possible at the time. The bottom line is this: the leader and those who follow choose to obey the truths they do know, and to submit to the One in charge of those they don't know.

6

Offenses

The Almighty has His own purposes. "Woe unto the world because of offences! for it must needs be that offences come; but woe to that man by whom the offence cometh!" If we shall suppose that American Slavery is one of those offences which, in the providence of God, must needs come, but which, having continued through His appointed time, He now wills to remove, and that He gives to both North and South, this terrible war as the woe due to those by whom the offence came, shall we discern therein any departure from those divine attributes which the believers in a Living God always ascribe to Him?

Offenses, no matter their origin, severity, or duration never obliterate righteousness. The definition of *righteousness* as it is used here is, *morally upright and uplifting relationships and actions based on enduring principle, designed to bring about positive results.* Offenses will be rectified by righteous people who subscribe to enduring standards and who act in accordance with them.

Within this portion of the Second Inaugural Address Lincoln unreservedly declared his personal belief: *"The Almighty has His own purposes."* In the concluding words of this section he employed a question of supposition to make the argument that offenses will not dissuade divine objectives, that no one should depart from a firm belief in God and His plans, even though severe struggle or war become the means to see those designs come to fruition.

Again Lincoln quoted scripture. The sentence he used comes from the New Testament, Matthew 18:7. Contextually these words, attributed to be those of Jesus, read as follows from verse 1 through verse 11 (Lincoln's quote is in italics):

"[1]At the same time came the disciples unto Jesus, saying, Who is the greatest in the kingdom of heaven? [2]And Jesus called a little child unto him, and set him in the midst of them, [3]And said, Verily I say unto you, Except ye be converted, and become as little children, ye shall not enter into the kingdom of heaven. [4]Whosoever therefore shall humble himself as this little child, the same is greatest in the kingdom of heaven. [5]And whoso shall receive one such little child in my name receiveth me. [6]But whoso shall offend one of these little ones which believe in me, it were better for him that a millstone were hanged about his neck, and that he were drowned in the depth of the sea. [7]*Woe unto the world because of offences! for it must needs be that offences come; but woe to that man by whom the offence cometh!* [8]Wherefore if thy hand or thy foot offend thee, cut them off, and cast them from thee: it is better for thee to enter into life halt or maimed, rather than having two hands or two feet to be cast into everlasting fire. [9]And if thine eye offend thee, pluck it out, and cast it from thee: it is better for thee to enter into life with one eye, rather than having two eyes to be cast into hell fire. [10]Take heed that ye despise not one of these little ones; for I say unto you, That in heaven their angels do always behold the face of my Father which is in heaven. [11]For the Son of man is come to save that which was lost."

Lincoln's use of the passage was contextually correct though the truths within these words can be difficult for some to embrace. One theme of the passage is the contrast between good and bad actions and the consequences of each. Another theme is that choices exist for those who offend. Offenders who pinpoint the sources of their tendencies that cause offense can and should weigh their destructive behaviors and choose right instead of wrong. Still another theme is that offending defenseless people (in this case, "little ones" referring to children, those who clearly cannot defend themselves, or those whose humility is like a child's) carries even greater judgment.

The primary point in Lincoln's use of the sentence was this: offenses will come and they will produce negative consequences. There is no doubt of the truth of this. Accountability rests in the causes of offenses where motive and method are determined and chosen. The implied truth is that the one who causes an offense will receive judgment, the "woe," because that person is culpable and merits blame if not punishment. The topic of justice, though the word is not mentioned, is in evidence here.

Justice will be served. Consider the words of Emerson quoted in *Leadership Is—How to Build Your Legacy*, from an edition of *Essays: First Series* (1841), "Emerson has stated, 'Every act rewards itself… Cause and effect, means and ends, seed and fruit, cannot be severed; for the effect already blooms in the cause, the end preexists in the means, the fruit in the seed… The nature and soul of things takes on itself the guaranty of the fulfillment of every contract, so that honest service cannot come to loss… Every stroke shall be repaid…'

"As Emerson has explained, proper rewards, commensurate in scope and degree of likeness of character because they are based on the Laws of Sowing and Reaping, and Compensation will assuredly come in time. This promise is guaranteed, its system has repeated itself since memory began."

In postmodern phraseology: "What goes around comes around", even though many who use this phrase may not understand its magnitude.

Lincoln postulated that in the great trial of the Civil War both North and South were receiving God's providential justice as due consequence of allowing American slavery to exist. Lincoln said that although God's will may have permitted slavery to exist anyway, the payment for the awful offense once it came was to be seen in the immense sacrifices of life and property in the Civil War. In the final analysis this recompense was far greater in scope than anyone could ever have imagined.

Woe is a word not used much anymore, though it may be heard occasionally as a cry of desperation: "Woe is me!" A definition of this word is in order. From *Merriam-Webster's 11th Collegiate Dictionary*, *woe* is "1 : a condition of deep suffering from misfortune, affliction, or grief; 2 : ruinous trouble." The Civil War constituted epic and deadly woe.

The battle of Gettysburg produced great destruction of human life and property. Photographic images of the battlefield were taken as early as July 5th as the Army of Northern Virginia retreated, pursued by Meade's Army of the Potomac. Though both armies had departed, the devastation they left behind on the fields and forests was immense. One particular photograph purported to have been taken near the Rose Farm, shows a fallen soldier disemboweled with a severed hand by his side. Originally described as an image of death from a shell, a more likely story is that the soldier's body had been mutilated by a wandering pig. According to National Park Historian John Heiser, Gettysburg National Military Park, "That the damage to this body was done by a roaming hog is a theory put forth by author William Frassanito but we also know that the troops who moved through this site were subjected to artillery fire from Union batteries at the Peach Orchard, several of which reported using solid shot against enemy formations. The hog story is just one explanation of the mutilated body."

This photo and other images of death graphically illustrated the loneliness and isolation of combat. Before the advent of Civil War photography, Americans had never really seen the personal sides of waging war and taking life. These pictures introduced the public to the sorrow and immense woe of war.

Leaders and followers of both armies understood that sacrifice and death were parts of the mission in which they were engaged. They knew that some of the soldiers who were present on one morning would not return that same evening. They understood that others might come back but be forever maimed from injuries wrought by the armaments of the day.

In my office I display a small collection of Confederate and Union bullets, called Minié balls. These were taken from the battlefields of Gettysburg many years ago. Mementos like these are virtually impossible to find now unless new construction on private land unearths them. Relics are now not permitted to be retrieved and retained from any battlefield location owned and operated by the National Park Service.

What a story these tokens tell! Millions of these bullets were fired by both sides. Impact with flesh or bone produced disastrous effects. Though surgeons tried to aid the wounded, their practices of medicine and sanitation were far less than adequate. Infection was rampant. A battlefield just after the shooting had stopped harbored dead, dying, and severely wounded men, sprawled and suffering, victims of munitions that bore instant death or wrought prolonged agony.

Lessons of War

Stories of bravery and valor were born as bullets wreaked their destruction. One account is that of Colonel Isaac Avery who hailed from North Carolina. The following story is quoted from the National Park Service website, Gettysburg tour: "By the morning of July 2nd, East Cemetery Hill was one of the most heavily fortified positions on the field, its base ringed with infantry and three artillery batteries crowning the summit. The western slope of Cemetery Hill, where the Soldiers' National Cemetery is today, was also heavily fortified with infantry and artillery.

"Despite the hill's apparent invincibility, a Confederate attack briefly shattered the Union defenses here on July 2. Soon after dusk, the Confederate brigades of General Harry Hays and Colonel Isaac Avery began their charge from a stream bed on the Henry Culp Farm, crossing over a half-mile of rolling farmland, blocked out by low stone walls or high rail fences, each an obstacle to the advancing southerners.

"Losses for both sides were severe and among the seriously wounded was Colonel Avery…struck through the neck by a musket ball 'in front of the heights' of Cemetery Hill, where he was discovered after the charge by several of his soldiers and the 6th North Carolina's Major Tate. Tate knew the wound was mortal and provided everything he could to make Avery's last hours comfortable as he lay dying in a field hospital.

"Unable to speak, Avery scribbled a simple note for Tate: 'Tell my father I died with my face to the enemy.' Colonel Avery died following day. Command of the brigade was passed to Colonel

A. C. Godwin who in his report, eulogized his fellow officer: 'In his death the country lost one of her truest and bravest sons, and the army one of its most gallant and efficient officers.'"

The country had become weary of war long before the Second Inaugural Address was presented. Stories of death and devastation had become commonplace. Families on both sides had endured the woe to which Lincoln referred.

The president was convinced that only God knew when the Civil War would end. Lincoln did not venture to predict either time or victor. Far from creating a platform for denial of the actions of a just and righteous Almighty, Lincoln convincingly asked this question, "...*shall we discern therein any departure from those divine attributes which the believers in a Living God always ascribe to Him?*" Clearly the answer was, "No."

Leaders who see their organizations embroiled in conflict do well when they submit to Higher Authority while continuing to act to fulfill their righteous causes. This is especially true when the results of a conflict are at points unknown.

If you are the leader, embrace these principles:
- Remain focused on your righteous purpose.
- Complete your tasks to the best of your ability.
- In your desires for justice, place final results and judgments of men and means in the hands of God, that all shall be accomplished in accordance to His will.

7

Hope, Prayer, and Submission

Fondly do we hope—fervently do we pray—that this mighty scourge of war may speedily pass away. Yet, if God wills that it continue, until all the wealth piled by the bond-man's two hundred and fifty years of unrequited toil shall be sunk, and until every drop of blood drawn with the lash, shall be paid by another drawn with the sword, as was said three thousand years ago, so still it must be said "the judgments of the Lord, are true and righteous altogether."

Hoping and praying are united in the opening words of this section. Lincoln commonly used alliteration to make his points easier to recall. This technique is seen here in his use of the words *fondly* and *fervently*. Lincoln captures the attention of the listener with the phrase and declares a profound truth for one who trusts in God: hope and prayer are inseparable. Prayer without hope would be a meaningless exercise.

In the second sentence Lincoln links hope and prayer to an attitude of submission to the will of God. Another truth is revealed: the finite is best positioned to receive from The Infinite when the finite submits to powers that exceed its will and understanding.

Hope is a wish or a dream, but it is more. From *Core Teams Work Their Principles and Practices* Copyright 2007 by Glen Aubrey, page 96: "Here it constitutes a strong and continuing desire for the good, right, and true. Hope that does not disappoint, and is not disappointed, focuses and frames best results that may come to pass if enough diligent effort is put forth." Hope and prayer are connected. We hope, we wish, we dream, we pray, but we have to work for what we want. It will be up to God to fulfill our efforts according to His design and in His time.

Prayer is an expression of earnest desire offered to a Being greater than us. Wise leaders combine hope and prayer when faced with crises that are beyond their ability to solve. They realize that submission to Higher Authority is not optional and forms the foundation of fondest hopes and fervent prayers. Human understanding and powers are limited, like it or not. Simply put, people are not ultimately in charge. Great leaders know and respect this.

On February 27, 2005 I had the unique privilege of meeting

President and Mrs. George W. Bush. The following account of that event is quoted from *Industrial Strength Solutions Build Successful Work Teams!* by Glen Aubrey, Copyright 2006, beginning on page 39.

"We were visiting Washington, D.C. with dear friends, and were privileged to attend church services at St. John's Church, across the street from Lafayette Park. The service was to begin at 8:00 a.m., and we were told that President and Mrs. Bush might be in attendance that day. We were, of course, excited at this prospect, and arrived at the church a little before 7:00 a.m. It was unbelievably cold and I surmised that the Secret Service had compassion on us, allowing us to pass through security and get into the warm building perhaps sooner than anyone anticipated.

"There were six in our party and we were seated one row in back of another, three-and-three, about 10 rows from the front on an aisle. We realized that we were the only ones presently in the church, except for one Secret Service agent who sat two rows in back of us, and an occasional parade of other agents, White House staff, and a couple of ushers who moved through, up and down the aisles. As the clock neared 7:30 a.m. the church began to fill, and at about 7:50 a.m. the lone agent left his seat and knelt in the aisle by my side, greeted me warmly, and asked if my wife would kindly move her coat to the other side of our son, which I communicated to her, and she did. He thanked me, and left. Odd, I thought, but we were not ones to question at that point.

"Several minutes later, just before 8:00 a.m., Mrs. Bush,

followed by President Bush, entered from stage left (audience right) at the front of the church and greeted the clergy. My first thought was, 'They look just like they do on TV.' Duh. Only one other time had I had the opportunity to be in the same room with a president, actually George W. Bush's father, when he had come to San Diego to speak to our downtown Rotary club, and I only saw him from a distance away.

"Our assumption was that President and Mrs. Bush would sit toward the front of the church, so when they walked across the front, turned left and proceeded down the aisle toward us, we were startled, if not taken aback. But we were completely amazed when Mrs. Bush sat directly behind my wife, Cindy, and the President sat directly in back of me. I suddenly became acutely aware of the back of my head, and hoped my haircut and coat collar were okay! Understand that St. John's church was constructed in 1820, and that people may have been a little shorter back then, and that these pews had been placed very close together. To be that near a president dwarfed any other experience with notable folks I had ever met, let me tell you. In fact, in my talks since this event occurred, I am fond of saying that if you have ever had a leader breathe down your neck, I can top that!

"The service proceeded, and President and Mrs. Bush were fully engaged in the liturgy. From the Book of Common Prayer we were led, responded, quoted Scripture and prayed. As part of this outline we were presented with the opportunity to 'stand and greet one another' and all in our party gulped, then smiled.

Lessons of War

We rose and noticed that the first people the President and Mrs. Bush greeted warmly and with great enthusiasm were a group of teenagers sitting to our right, expressing engaged interest in them as would, well, people who were truly interested. Then we met the First Couple. Warm and gracious, they put us at ease as I introduced my family to them, and I noticed particularly how intentional President Bush was in his gaze, and firm in his handshake.

"The service progressed and the homily concluded, at which time the President addressed Laura and said, 'That was good,' (and it was). The congregation was given the option at this time of participating in a segment of the service called Communion.

"At this service the communion elements are served at an altar at the front of the church, and those who wish to partake file up to take their kneeling places there, to be served by two of the clergy, one with the wafer representing the body of Christ, and one with the wine, representing His blood shed for redemption of sin, the wine served from a common chalice.

"It came time for our row to proceed and we stood, as did the President and Mrs. Bush who were in back of us. Turning to him, I thought it only proper that I offer that he and Mrs. Bush proceed first, seeing that he is the most powerful man in the world, and his response was, 'No, no, you and your friends go first,' which we did. I mean, you don't really want to argue with a president, right?

"So I let my wife go first, followed by my son, and as I was about to proceed up the aisle as well, I felt a deliberate tugging at my right coat pocket, a pulling on the fabric that was clearly intentional. I looked quickly back and surmised immediately that it could be none other than George W. Bush—no one else was near. Indeed, it was he. My coat pocket flap had become tucked into the pocket, askew to the world, and he simply reached out—and fixed my coat. It was a moment.

"While knowing exactly what had happened I wasn't sure exactly why, but in looking into his face, was greeted by shining eyes and a huge grin. He said, verbatim, 'I just want you to look sharp going up there.' All I could do was smile and say, 'Why, thank you, Mr. President.' What would you say? Stunned as I was, and as I think about it still, I recall feelings now of a combination of gratitude, amazement, and light-hearted friendly encounter, all enveloped into one moment in time.

"We proceeded up to the front altar, and the President and I knelt side by side for communion. I was served first, and then we both bowed in silent prayer after taking the elements. One of the pictures that my wife carries in her mind and describes so well is that as she was finished praying she looked up, and will always remember seeing Glen Aubrey and the President of the United States kneeling together in prayer at an altar of communion.

"Clearly this is a great memory for us, and because there were no cameras, media, or other devices to record such a moment, the event lives and is cherished in our minds, and will for as long as our recollections last. What a privilege!

Lessons of War

"But there are lessons here, important leadership and teambuilding lessons. From that encounter forward I have reflected on them substantially and will highlight them here. See if they ring true in light of what you have just read:

1. Leadership that commands respect is fully engaged in and with the people who follow, regardless of station or status.
2. Leadership whole-heartedly participates through a team's function where strong relational values permeate understanding, and cooperation on behalf of a cause perpetuates right action.
3. Leadership is intentional and not distracted by nonessentials.
4. Leadership is complimentary.
5. Leadership is firm in its commitment toward a higher and worthwhile purpose.
6. Leadership looks for ways to make followers successful, even if it means invading. In the story above, simply making my coat look appropriate was a service rendered by the President that he did not have to do! He did it, though, for the reasons he stated, and I was the beneficiary.
7. Leadership is humble and submissive to a Creator and a Cause greater than self. Kneeling in prayer at an altar before God in obedience to His authority says much about the man and his wife, politics notwithstanding. Humble leaders serve to the best of their God-given abilities when

they recognize the Source from which their strength comes."

Submission to God rightly portrays meekness, strength under control. Superior leaders know that when they submit to Higher Authority they place themselves in the best position to create and participate in positive outcomes. Lincoln knew this, declared his submission to God, and trusted Him for the outcome as right principles were upheld and practiced.

Lincoln's hope and prayer were that the war would soon end. He realized the immensity of devastation already wrought and he sought to conclude the trial the country was enduring. In his speech he chose the word *scourge* to describe the conditions of the ongoing conflict and its effects. A scourge is more than an unwelcomed situation or result; it is a cause as well.

Scourges were evident throughout the entire crucible of Civil War conflict. One example at Gettysburg surrounds the story of a free black man, Abraham Bryan (also spelled Brian or Brien). Bryan owned and tilled a twelve-acre farm on Cemetery Ridge. This ridge became a strongly fortified Union line of defense during the second and third days of the battle.

Before the conflict invaded the town Bryan decided to depart the area so he would not be captured by Confederate forces and be re-enslaved. He abandoned his holdings with a hope of returning. During his absence his house suffered severe damage, mainly caused by the Union troops who occupied it.

Lessons of War

A photograph taken shortly after the battle shows some of the devastation to Bryan's property. The ruination was enormous. Windows were broken out, fences were leveled, and crops were destroyed by the fighting in the vicinity.

Following the war Bryan filed a claim with the federal government to recover damages to his home and lands in the amount of $1,028.00. Eventually he was awarded $15.00.

This man's story is only one account of the scourge of war. Bryan's experience is the tale of a man who, because of his race, feared his destiny. The battle swarmed around him and consumed his lands. He received little solace from a settlement of sorts, but at least he lived.

The war's effects produced other scourges on families who endured and practiced divided loyalties. Entire households were broken apart by the causes and demands of conflict. Stories of fathers, sons, brothers, and extended family relatives fighting on opposite sides were common. Positions of opposing parties engulfed a nation, separated kindred units, and widened rifts of opinion, belief, and practice that in some cases never were bridged.

Even Mary Lincoln, the wife of the president, was accused of disloyalty and treason. Many of her immediate and extended family were Southerners, and four of her brothers fought for the Confederacy. Three of them died in the war. Rumors of Mrs. Lincoln's supposed disloyalty were rampant, though eventually all were proven unfounded. Here's the truth: leaders know that gossip, lies, and groundless accusations often pervade a scourge that precedes and accompanies a conflict of wills.

Further, leaders are fully aware that a scourge of confrontation elicits powerful emotions. They understand that a curse of conflict can cause doubts which lead to mistrust. They appreciate that lingering effects of severed relations can endure for a very long time.

Effective leaders face these contingencies with earnest prayer enveloped in hope. They are willing to accept the fact that powers are in play beyond their control. They know that strength in these turbulent times often comes from submitting to the will of Higher Authority. One quote attributed to Lincoln is this: "I have been driven many times upon my knees by the overwhelming conviction that I had nowhere else to go."

In the passage of the Second Inaugural above, Lincoln drew comparisons and used language his audiences would have understood well. The contrasts he employed were poignant: "... *until all the wealth piled by the bond-man's two hundred and fifty years of unrequited toil shall be sunk, and until every drop of blood drawn with the lash, shall be paid by another drawn with the sword...*" Sacrifices of toil and slavery were compared to the horrifying amount of blood spilt by the cruel armaments of the Civil War.

"*Yet, if God wills...*" His use of the word *if* firmly declared that in these considerations God was in control and that His judgments would remain true and righteous. The "*if*" proclaimed that conditions of conflict and resolution were subject to plans that exceeded the limits of human understanding.

Lincoln had postulated that the will of God alone would conclude the conflict or extend it. His reference to *"three thousand years ago"* was yet another drawn from scripture. He quoted: *"the judgments of the Lord, are true and righteous altogether."* This passage comes from Psalm 19 in the Old Testament. In context it reads like this, beginning with verse 7 (the passage Lincoln quoted is in italics):

"[7]The law of the LORD is perfect, converting the soul: the testimony of the LORD is sure, making wise the simple. [8]The statutes of the LORD are right, rejoicing the heart: the commandment of the LORD is pure, enlightening the eyes. [9]The fear of the LORD is clean, enduring for ever: *the judgments of the LORD are true and righteous altogether.*"

Though fondness of hope and earnest prayer should be offered from heartfelt desires to see the end of war and relief from its scourge, ultimately a conflict's cessation rests in the hands of God alone. Lincoln emphasized the abiding aspect of God's control over human affairs in his use of the word *must*: "… *so still it must be said…*" He showed that human beings who live in truth recognize their limitations and possess no alternative but submission to the designs of The Almighty.

Great leaders understand that they are not ultimately in control, that only God decides and designs a beginning and an end. Fully righteous judgment cannot be rendered if the entire picture cannot be known, and rarely within human capability can a full picture be ascertained.

An application for any leader: try to obtain all available facts before rendering a decision whose choice will affect not only outcomes, but the lives of people who must live within its results. Understand that only upon the basis of complete facts can an accurate decision and choice be made. Also understand that you may have to make a decision even when all the facts are not known and any choice you make will affect others who must live within the consequences of your choice. In these circumstances a great leader looks to God for higher and more complete wisdom.

8

Firmness in the Right

With malice toward none; with charity for all; with firmness in the right, as God gives us to see the right...

Malice is a strong word. Again from *Merriam-Webster's 11th Collegiate Dictionary*, "1 : desire to cause pain, injury, or distress to another; 2 : intent to commit an unlawful act or cause harm without legal justification or excuse; MALICE implies a deep-seated often unexplainable desire to see another suffer."

Lincoln sought to erase all of it. He wanted to replace deep-seated desires to impose suffering with nobler acts of charity. While there remained a job to do, to reunite the Union, the methods chosen to conclude the war would emerge from core desires of peace and forgiveness. He would refuse abiding retribution and punitive subjugation.

Lincoln's desire for *"malice toward none"* and *"charity for all"* played out at Appomattox when Lee surrendered to Grant. The story is widely known that Lieutenant-General Grant offered generous terms to General Robert E. Lee and the Confederate army.

The surrender was recalled by Grant twenty years after the event. Lee had died in 1870 and Grant passed away in 1885. As Grant's health failed he wrote his *Personal Memoirs of Ulysses S. Grant* (New York, 1885) which was published in the year of his death. Quoted from his memoirs on pages 555-560, note the tone of magnanimity and generosity beginning with a letter that Grant wrote to Lee on April 9th. That letter is followed by Grant's commentary.

>Appomattox C. H., Va.,
>Ap'l 9th, 1865
>
>Gen. R. E. Lee,
>Comd'g C. S. A.
>
>Gen.:
>
>In accordance with the substance of my letter to you of the 8th inst., I propose to receive the surrender of the Army of N. Va. on the following terms, to wit: Rolls of all the officers and men to

be made in duplicate. One copy to be given to an officer designated by me, the other to be retained by such officer or officers as you may designate. The officers to give their individual paroles not to take up arms against the Government of the United States until properly exchanged, and each company or regimental commander sign a like parole for the men of their commands. The arms, artillery and public property to be parked and stacked, and turned over to the officer appointed by me to receive them. This will not embrace the side-arms of the officers, nor their private horses or baggage. This done, each officer and man will be allowed to return to their homes, not to be disturbed by United States authority so long as they observe their paroles and the laws in force where they may reside.

Very respectfully,
U.S. Grant,
Lt.-Gen.

"When I put my pen to the paper I did not know the first word that I should make use of in writing the terms. I only knew what was in my mind, and I wished to express it clearly, so that there could be no mistaking it. As I wrote on, the thought occurred to me that the officers had their own private horses and effects, which were important to them, but of no value to us; also that it would be an unnecessary humiliation to call upon them to deliver their side arms.

"No conversation, not one word, passed between General Lee and myself, either about private property, side arms, or kindred subjects. He appeared to have no objections to the terms first proposed; or if he had a point to make against them he wished to wait until they were in writing to make it. When he read over that part of the terms about side arms, horses and private property of the officers, he remarked, with some feeling, I thought, that this would have a happy effect upon his army.

"Then, after a little further conversation, General Lee remarked to me again that their army was organized a little differently from the army of the United States (still maintaining by implication that we were two countries); that in their army the cavalrymen and artillerists owned their own horses; and he asked if he was to understand that the men who so owned their horses were to be permitted to retain them. I told him that as the terms were written they would not; that only the officers were permitted to take their private property. He then, after reading over the terms a second time, remarked that that was clear.

"I then said to him that I thought this would be about the last battle of the war—I sincerely hoped so; and I said further I took it that most of the men in the ranks were small farmers. The whole country had been so raided by the two armies that it was doubtful whether they would be able to put in a crop to carry themselves and their families through the next winter without the aid of the horses they were then riding. The United States did not want them and I would, therefore, instruct the officers I left behind to receive the paroles of his troops to let every man of the Confederate army who claimed to own a horse or mule take the animal to his home. Lee remarked again that this would have a happy effect.

"He then sat down and wrote out the following letter:

Headquarters Army of Northern Virginia,
April 9, 1865

Lieut.-General U. S. Grant.

General:

—I received your letter of this date containing the terms of the surrender of the Army of Northern Virginia as proposed by you. As they are substantially the same as those expressed in your letter of the 8th inst., they are accepted. I will proceed to designate the proper officers to carry the stipulations into effect.

R. E. Lee,
General

"While duplicates of the two letters were being made, the Union generals present were severally presented to General Lee.

"The much talked of surrendering of Lee's sword and my handing it back, this and much more that has been said about it is the purest romance. The word sword or side arms was not mentioned by either of us until I wrote it in the terms. There was no premeditation, and it did not occur to me until the moment I wrote it down. If I had happened to omit it, and General Lee had called my attention to it, I should have put it in the terms precisely as I acceded to the provision about the soldiers retaining their horses.

"General Lee, after all was completed and before taking his leave, remarked that his army was in a very bad condition for want of food, and that they were without forage; that his men had been living for some days on parched corn exclusively, and that he would have to ask me for rations and forage. I told him 'certainly,' and asked for how many men he wanted rations. His answer was 'about twenty-five thousand': and I authorized him to send his own commissary and quartermaster to Appomattox Station, two or three miles away, where he could have, out of the trains we had stopped, all the provisions wanted. As for forage, we had ourselves depended almost entirely upon the country for that.

"Generals Gibbon, Griffin and Merritt were designated by me to carry into effect the paroling of Lee's troops before they should start for their homes—General Lee leaving Generals Longstreet, Gordon and Pendleton for them to confer with in order to facilitate this work. Lee and I then separated as cordially as we had met, he returning to his own lines, and all went into bivouac for the night at Appomattox.

"Soon after Lee's departure I telegraphed to Washington as follows:

Headquarters Appomattox C. H., Va.,
April 9th, 1865, 4:30 p.m.

Hon. E. M. Stanton:
Secretary of War,
Washington.

General Lee surrendered the Army of Northern Virginia this afternoon on terms proposed by myself. The accompanying additional correspondence will show the conditions fully.

U. S. Grant,
Lieut.-General

"When news of the surrender first reached our lines our men commenced firing a salute of a hundred guns in honor of the victory. I at once sent word, however, to have it stopped. The Confederates were now our prisoners, and we did not want to exult over their downfall."

Lessons of War

Exercising charity toward a defeated foe requires more than just obedience to orders. True intentions have to proceed from the heart if they are to be performed with integrity. This kind of forbearance requires extending kindness and forgiveness whether thought to be deserved or not. This kind of compassion surpasses human understanding and will.

Two years earlier at Gettysburg, malice was replaced by care as the battle waged and upon its conclusion. On page 43 of *At Gettysburg or What a Girl Saw and Heard of the Battle—A True Narrative* are found Tillie's descriptions of what she first saw of wounded Union soldiers who began to arrive at the Weikert's home toward the end of the first day's battle. Remember, at the time Tillie was about fifteen years old.

"It was toward the close of the afternoon of this day that some of the wounded from the field of battle began to arrive where I was staying. They reported hard fighting, many wounded and killed, and were afraid our troops would be defeated and perhaps routed.

"The first wounded soldier whom I met had his thumb tied up. This I thought was dreadful, and told him so.

"'Oh,' said he, 'this is nothing; you'll see worse than this before long.'

"'Oh! I hope not,' I innocently replied.

"Soon two officers carrying their arms in slings made their appearance, and I more fully began to realize that something terrible had taken place.

"Now the wounded began to come in greater numbers. Some limping, some with their heads and arms in bandages, some crawling, others carried on stretchers or brought in ambulances. Suffering, cast down and dejected, it was a truly pitiable gathering. Before night the barn was filled with the shattered and dying heroes of this day's struggle."

During the battle in and around Gettysburg thousands of men from both sides were shot. At a time of immense distrust and even hatred, human compassion was still demonstrated for the wounded and hurting of both sides.

Most public buildings and churches of Gettysburg were turned into field hospitals. One such facility served as a hospital for both Union and Confederate soldiers. This was the High Street or "Common" School, an imposing two story brick structure that still stands to this day. Built in 1847, it was Gettysburg's first consolidated public school building. According to the plaque positioned in front of the building, "…the school became a hospital on July 1, 1863, when Union wounded began arriving from the battlefield. By evening it housed Union and Confederate casualties, separated by floors. The school building was well suited for the task but the location was exposed to the constant fighting between skirmish lines in front of Cemetery Hill. The result was unnerving, but not life threatening." One of the 17th Connecticut infantryman recalled, "…bullets… rattling against our hospital, making a great racket." And another interesting piece, "At the battle's end a Union soldier, hiding in the school's bell cupola since being cut off during the retreat on July 1st, emerged to enjoy his first meal in three days." One can only wonder what the wounded from both sides felt knowing that only a ceiling or floor separated them, but that they were receiving aid, regardless.

The second half of the portion of the Second Inaugural we are considering states, "...*with firmness in the right, as God gives us to see the right...*" The leadership truths of this phrase must be extrapolated. Lincoln was dedicated to putting the United States back together. He was firm in his determination to accomplish this goal, because he believed it was right.

Lincoln used historical precedent to prove his belief. When Lincoln delivered his First Inaugural Address on March 4, 1861, he stated: "*The Union is much older than the Constitution. It was formed, in fact, by the Articles of Association in 1774. It was matured and continued by the Declaration of Independence in 1776. It was further matured, and the faith of all the then thirteen States expressly plighted and engaged that it should be perpetual, by the Articles of Confederation in 1778. And finally, in 1787, one of the declared objects for ordaining and establishing the Constitution was to form a more perfect Union.*"

A "*more perfect Union*" had been designed to stand for all time. Lincoln was convinced that he was correct in his interpretation of the country's perpetuity. In the Second Inaugural he positioned his understanding of *right* in submission to God once again with, "...*the right, as God gives us to see the right...*"

These are meaningful words. In context they declare that it

was God Who gave humankind the capability to ascertain right from wrong. Where right was to be determined, as in the case of the perpetuity of the Union, God was seen to be its author. God would offer the comprehensive wisdom to know right from wrong as a gift to those who sought to follow His precepts..

Lasting leadership principles are embedded here. One that is implied is that some people sincerely believe they are right when indeed they are very wrong. Another is that great leadership determines what is correct based upon wisdom higher than humans can craft. To definitively know the *right* one must seek the gifts of abiding truth and understanding, and base moral decisions and choices upon them. Seen in the context of his speech where he quoted scripture repeatedly it is reasonable to conclude that Lincoln believed a foundation for defining, understanding, and doing *right* was to be found in Biblical truth.

9

Finish the Work

...let us strive on to finish the work we are in; to bind up the nation's wounds; to care for him who shall have borne the battle, and for his widow, and his orphan—

The North had to prevail if the Union was to be preserved. Finishing the work meant winning the war. Lincoln was committed to achieving this result.

The road to Appomattox was not easy. The leaders of both armies were determined to win. While correspondence between Lieutenant-General Grant and General Lee that began on April 7, 1865 set the stage for surrender, these exchanges illustrate the commitment both commanders exercised as they determined to pursue their own courses toward victory.

The following letters were extracted from the *Report of Lieut. Gen. Ulysses S. Grant, U. S. Army, commanding Armies of the United States, The Richmond (Virginia) Campaign from the Official Records of the War of the Rebellion, 1880-1901.* Note the reticence first expressed on the part of Lee, the determination on the part of Grant, and Lee's eventual and dignified capitulation. Note also how both men wanted to avoid "any further effusion of blood."

At this time Grant's army was ruthlessly pursuing Lee's army. Under these conditions both men reached the understanding that peace through surrender was more desirable than continual and devastating bloodshed. They realized that the conflict could end if they could cooperate and design a conclusion upon which they both agreed.

Another leadership principle is here: cooperation based upon what is agreed can lead to cessation of conflict. The directive is this: build upon what you agree, not upon what you do not agree.

APRIL 7, 1865

General R. E. LEE:

GENERAL: The result of the last week must convince you of the hopelessness of further resistance on the part of the Army of Northern Virginia in this struggle. I feel that it is so, and regard it as my duty to shift from myself the responsibility of any further effusion of blood, by asking of you the surrender of that portion of the C. S. Army known as the Army of Northern Virginia.

U.S. GRANT,
Lieutenant-General

HEADQUARTERS ARMY OF NORTHERN VIRGINIA,
APRIL 7, 1865

Lieut. Gen. U.S. GRANT:

GENERAL: I have received your note of this date. Though not entertaining the opinion you express on the hopelessness of further resistance on the part of the Army of Northern Virginia, I reciprocate your desire to avoid useless effusion of blood, and therefore, before considering your proposition, ask the terms you will offer on condition of its surrender.

R. E. LEE,
General.

Glen Aubrey

APRIL 8, 1865

General R. E. LEE:

GENERAL: Your note of last evening, in reply to mine of same date, asking the condition on which I will accept the surrender of the Army of Northern Virginia, is just received. In reply I would say that, peace being my great desire, there is but one condition I would insist upon, namely, that the men and officers surrendered shall be disqualified for taking up arms again against the Government of the United States until properly exchanged. I will meet you, or will designate officers to meet any officers you may name for the same purpose, at any point agreeable to you, for the purpose of arranging definitely the terms upon which the surrender of the Army of Northern Virginia will be received.

U.S. GRANT,
Lieutenant-General.

Lessons of War

HEADQUARTERS ARMY OF NORTHERN VIRGINIA,
APRIL 8, 1865

Lieut. Gen. U.S. GRANT:

GENERAL: I received at a late hour your note of to-day. In mine of yesterday I did not intend to propose the surrender of the Army of Northern Virginia, but to ask the terms of your proposition. To be frank, I do not think the emergency has arisen to call for the surrender of this army, but as the restoration of peace should be the sole object of all, I desired to know whether your proposals would lead to that end. I cannot, therefore, meet you with a view to surrender the Army of Northern Virginia, but as far as your proposal may affect the C. S. forces under my command, and tend to the restoration of peace, I should be pleased to meet you at 10 a.m., to-morrow; on the old stage road to Richmond, between the picket-lines of the two armies.

R. E. LEE,
General.

APRIL 9, 1865

General R. E. LEE:

GENERAL: Your note of yesterday is received. I have no authority to treat on the subject of peace; the meeting proposed for 10 a.m. to-day could lead to no good. I will state, however, general, that I am equally anxious for peace with yourself, and the whole North entertains the same feeling. The terms upon which peace can be had are well understood. By the South laying down their arms they will hasten that most desirable event, save thousands of human lives, and hundreds of millions of property not yet destroyed. Seriously hoping that all our difficulties may be settled without the loss of another life, I subscribe myself, etc.,

U.S. GRANT,
Lieutenant-General.

HEADQUARTERS ARMY OF NORTHERN VIRGINIA,
APRIL 9, 1865

Lieut. Gen. U.S. GRANT:

GENERAL: I received your note of this morning on the picket-line, whither I had come to meet you and ascertain definitely what terms were embraced in your proposal of yesterday with reference to the surrender of this army. I now ask an interview in accordance with the offer contained in your letter of yesterday for that purpose.

R. E. LEE,
General.

APRIL 9, 1865

General R. E. LEE:

GENERAL: Your note of this date is but this moment (11:50 A.M.) received, in consequence of my having passed from the Richmond and Lynchburg road to the Farmville and Lynchburg road. I am at this writing about four miles west of Walker's Church, and will push forward to the front for the purpose of meeting you. Notice sent to me on this road where you wish the interview to take place.

U.S. GRANT,
Lieutenant-General.

The surrender took place in the McLean House in the small town of Appomattox Court House, Virginia. The story of the family who owned the house is a curious one. The McLeans lived near the Bull Run or Manassas battlefield during the war's early years. In July, 1861 the First Battle of Bull Run was fought on the McLean farm.

Following the battle General P. G. T. Beauregard wrote, "A comical effect of this artillery fight was the destruction of the dinner of myself and staff by a Federal shell that fell into the fireplace of my headquarters at the McLean House." To avoid further risk and prevent the armies of North and South from decimating their farmland the McLean family moved to Appomattox Court House in 1863.

In light of the impending surrender (April, 1865) Lee sent a messenger to Appomattox Court House to find a location to meet. The messenger visited the McLean home and requested the use of the home for the proceedings. On April 9th the surrender occurred in the McLean's parlor. Later, McLean is supposed to have said, "The war began in my front yard and ended in my front parlor."

Though the McLeans may have sought to avert conflict and promote their own wellbeing, the conflict came to them anyway. The fact that the war ended in their parlor must have been a fitting conclusion. Leaders must remember that when conflict comes, it must not be avoided. It has to be dealt with and sometimes very close to home.

Winning is always attended by an aftermath. Conquering includes decisions and choices made by the victorious side.

Lincoln words *"to bind up the nation's wounds"* represented acts of healing as the goal of reuniting the country was commenced and achieved. Moving from war to peace was not easy or swift. Conflict waged even as the Second Inaugural Address was being delivered. Even after the surrender at Appomattox, armies fought, sacrifice mounted, and suffering remained. Despite these trying circumstances, Lincoln remained focused and looked toward an end of the war where true restoration could begin.

A plaque adorns the outside of the Department of Veterans Affairs in Washington, D.C. Quoting from Lincoln's Second Inaugural it reads:

> TO CARE FOR HIM WHO SHALL
> HAVE BORNE THE BATTLE AND
> FOR HIS WIDOW, AND HIS ORPHAN
> A. LINCOLN

Many soldiers had borne the battle. Thousands had been killed. Families mourned horrific losses all across North and South. Effects contributed to bitter feelings long after the war was concluded. Wounds like these are hard to heal. Some never do.

Lincoln believed that only with complete victory could chances for lasting healing and restoration even start. He realized what other leaders must as conflict is borne and transformed into winning or losing: victory carries tremendous responsibilities beyond conquest. One is to treat a scourge and its wounds with compassion and kindness when parties are no longer fighting.

Events following the surrender of Lee to Grant demonstrated noble attributes which Lincoln had longed for and beautifully expressed in his Second Inaugural Address. Though not everyone agreed, expressions from leaders of both armies marked surrender with honor, duty with gratitude, wrongs with reconciliation, and conquest with respect. These intangible merits were evidenced through meritorious words and deeds. They comprised the beginning points of restoration and unity. These were the essential elements of binding up the nation's wounds.

On April 10, 1865, Robert E. Lee gave his farewell address to his army. Observe the factors and the emotions that accompanied his words. Lee expressed resignation, resolute confidence, awareness of conditions, satisfaction with his army's efforts, a request for God's blessing, and immense gratitude.

> Headquarters, Army of Northern Virginia,
>
> 10th April 1865.
>
> After four years of arduous service marked by unsurpassed courage and fortitude, the Army of Northern Virginia has been compelled to yield to overwhelming numbers and resources.
>
> I need not tell the survivors of so many hard fought battles, who have remained steadfast to the

last, that I have consented to the result from no distrust of them.

But feeling that valor and devotion could accomplish nothing that could compensate for the loss that must have attended the continuance of the contest, I have determined to avoid the useless sacrifice of those whose past services have endeared them to their countrymen.

By the terms of the agreement, officers and men can return to their homes and remain until exchanged. You will take with you the satisfaction that proceeds from the consciousness of duty faithfully performed, and I earnestly pray that a merciful God will extend to you his blessing and protection.

With an unceasing admiration of your constancy and devotion to your Country, and a grateful remembrance of your kind and generous consideration for myself, I bid you an affectionate farewell.

– R. E. Lee, General, General Order No. 9

On that same day a six-man commission met to discuss a formal ceremony of surrender. Brig. General Joshua Chamberlain was the Union officer selected to lead the ceremony. Later he wrote this description of the event in *Passing of the Armies*, pages 260-261: "The momentous meaning of this occasion impressed me deeply. I resolved to mark it by some token of recognition, which could be no other than a salute of arms. Well aware of the responsibility assumed, and of the criticisms that would follow, as the sequel proved, nothing of that kind could move me in the least. The act could be defended, if needful, by the suggestion that such a salute was not to the cause for which the flag of the Confederacy stood, but to its going down before the flag of the Union.

"My main reason, however, was one for which I sought no authority nor asked forgiveness. Before us in proud humiliation stood the embodiment of manhood: men whom neither toils and sufferings, nor the fact of death, nor disaster, nor hopelessness could bend from their resolve; standing before us now, thin, worn, and famished, but erect, and with eyes looking level into ours, waking memories that bound us together as no other bond;— was not such manhood to be welcomed back into a Union so tested and assured?

"Instructions had been given; and when the head of each division column comes opposite our group, our bugle sounds the signal and instantly our whole line from right to left, regiment by regiment in succession, gives the soldier's salutation, from the "order arms" to the old "carry"—the marching salute. Gordon at the head of the column, riding with heavy spirit and downcast face, catches the sound of shifting arms, looks up, and, taking the meaning, wheels superbly, making with himself and his horse one uplifted figure, with profound salutation as he drops the point of his sword to the boot toe; then facing to his own command, gives word for his successive brigades to pass us with the same position of the manual,—honor answering honor. On our part not a sound of trumpet more, nor roll of drum; not a cheer, nor word nor whisper of vain-glorying, nor motion of man standing again at the order, but an awed stillness rather, and breath-taking, as if it were the passing of the dead!"

Whenever a death occurs—of a cause, of a dearly beloved person—fitting tributes should remember and honor the departed. These expressions should also refocus the attentions of those who remain onto the abiding principles and practices needed to fulfill current responsibilities and achieve future goals. Dignity, honor, respect, and lasting determination rank high among the traits of victors who care for those who have lost and suffered while they continue to accomplish their required responsibilities.

Wars are part of the human experience.

We know we must enter them.

We know how to win them.

Let us learn how to end them well.

This isn't just about victory and defeat. This is about ending well. This is about aligning with the right and true to achieve a peace that lasts beyond the crucibles of conflict and the consequences of war.

10

A Just and a Lasting Peace

...to do all which may achieve and cherish a just, and a lasting peace, among ourselves, and with all nations.

The 75th and last Civil War reunion occurred from June 29th through July 6th, 1938, at Gettysburg. A book commemorating the event, *The Last Reunion of the Blue and Gray*, written by Paul L. Roy, Gettysburg, Pennsylvania, copyrighted in 1950 by the author, was published and distributed by The Bookmart of Gettysburg, Pennsylvania. In its opening lines it claims to be "the only official and authentic story" of that historic occasion. This little book is a worthwhile read. According to the Foreword, the reunion was attended by 1,845 Veterans of the Civil War, 1,359 from the

North, and 486 from the South.

On July 3rd President Franklin Delano Roosevelt spoke for nine minutes to a crowd estimated to number 250,000 people as he dedicated the Eternal Light Peace Memorial located on the crest of Oak Ridge. To view a pdf version of the president's remarks, noted to be "a copy of the one he used on the platform" including several corrections he made in his own handwriting as well as his signature, please visit this website: http://www.gettysburgdaily.com/files/speechofthepresident.pdf.

The president's words delivered on this occasion were powerful. Here is the text:

SPEECH OF THE PRESIDENT
GETTYSBURG
JULY 3, 1938.

"Governor Earle, Veterans of the Blue and Gray, on behalf of the people of the United States I accept this monument in the spirit of brotherhood and peace.

"Immortal deeds and immortal words have created here a shrine of American patriotism. We are encompassed by 'The last full measure of devotion' of many men and by the words in which Abraham Lincoln expressed the simple faith for which they died.

Lessons of War

"It seldom helps to wonder how a statesman of one generation would surmount the crisis of another. A statesman deals with concrete difficulties—with things which must be done from day to day. Not often can he frame conscious patterns for the far off future.

"But the fullness of the stature of Lincoln's nature and the fundamental conflict which events forced upon his Presidency, invite us ever to turn to him for help.

"For the issue which he restated on this spot seventy-five years ago will be the continuing issue before this nation so long as we cling to the purposes for which it was founded—to preserve under the changing conditions of each generation a people's government for the people's good.

"The task assumes different shapes at different times. Sometimes the threat to popular government comes from political interests, sometimes from economic interests; sometimes we have to beat off all of them together.

"But the challenge is always the same—whether each generation facing its own circumstances can summon the practical devotion to attain and retain that greatest good for the greatest number which this government of the people was created to ensure.

"Lincoln spoke in solace for all who fought upon this field; and the years have laid their balm upon its wounds. Men who wore the Blue and men who wore the Gray are here together, a fragment spared by time. They are brought here by the memories of old divided loyalties, but they meet here in united loyalty to a united cause which the unfolding years have made it easier to see.

"All of them we honor, not asking under which Flag they fought then—thankful that they stand together under one Flag now.

"Lincoln was commander-in-chief in this old battle; he wanted above all things to be commander-in-chief of the new peace. He understood that battle there must be; that when a challenge to constituted government is thrown down, the people must in self-defense take it up; that the fight must be fought through to a decision so clear that it is accepted as being beyond recall.

"But Lincoln also understood that after such a decision, a democracy should seek peace through a new unity. For a democracy can keep alive only if the settlement of old difficulties clears the ground and transfers energies to face new responsibilities. Never can it have as much ability and purpose as it needs in that striving; the end of battle does not

Lessons of War

end the infinity of those needs.

"That is why Lincoln—commander of a people as well as of an army—asked that his battle end 'with malice toward none, with charity for all'.

"To the hurt of those who came after him, Lincoln's plea was long denied. A generation passed before the new unity became accepted fact.

"In later years new needs arose, and with them new tasks, worldwide in their perplexities, their bitterness and their modes of strife. Here in our land we give thanks that, avoiding war, we seek our ends through the peaceful processes of popular government under the Constitution.

"It is another conflict, as fundamental as Lincoln's, fought not with glint of steel, but with appeals to reason and justice on a thousand fronts—seeking to save for our common country opportunity and security for citizens in a free society.

"We are near to winning this battle. In its winning and through the years may we live by the wisdom and the humanity of the heart of Abraham Lincoln."

—Franklin D. Roosevelt

This great reunion symbolized a just and lasting peace that Americans had worked to achieve *"among ourselves,"* though as Roosevelt noted, "To the hurt of those who came after him, Lincoln's plea was long denied. A generation passed before the new unity became accepted fact."

Those who attended the anniversary cherished their history, their peaceful coexistence, the reunification of their country, and the values the commemorative event recalled. Elderly and honored veterans from formerly opposing sides shook hands in a demonstration of brotherhood at a place called The Angle, located near the High Water Mark of the Confederacy on Cemetery Ridge. This ground is sacred to the memory of combatants who fought there and the friendships they showed there. Their demonstration of unity portrayed their firm commitments to a greater cause than the conflict which had divided them. If you visit this location, pause a moment to be thankful.

In 1863, at Gettysburg, Lincoln set the framework for crafting a just and last peace within his war torn country. He concluded his Gettysburg Address with these words: *"It is rather for us to be here dedicated to the great task remaining before us—that from these honored dead we take increased devotion to that cause for which they gave the last full measure of devotion—that we here highly resolve that these dead shall not have died in vain—that this nation, under God, shall have a new birth of freedom—and that government of the people, by the people, for the people, shall not perish from the earth."*

The new birth of freedom Lincoln referred to would usher

in the opportunity for unified peace. The people of this nation would birth that peace and sustain it. The people were responsible, along with their elected government, to reunite their country, preserve their unity, and protect their freedom.

Events at Gettysburg, on and off the battlefield, illustrated leadership based on abiding truth, truth that prepared the thinking and actions of a nation, to craft and accept a fitting conclusion to the Civil War. Gettysburg in 1863—the place, the battle, and the address—charted the course toward Appomattox when in 1865 the Civil War came to its close.

Leaders do well to learn the enduring lessons of these times. Great leaders who face conflict today should be students of exemplary leaders of yesterday. As students they will learn to base their actions upon enduring principle, hold on to what is right no matter the odds, pave the paths of peace with victory and charity, and celebrate restoration within bonds of lasting unity.

Acts of leadership and heroism demonstrated during the Gettysburg campaign showed that military or civilian leaders, regardless of rank, age, title, position, or place responded to the crises of their time with enduring principles of all time, to produce right and sustainable results. History's models of effective leadership help leaders of today face contemporary conflicts well, if they pay attention to these lessons and embrace them. Eternal ideals and the ideas they engender form solid and lasting results when applied to any confrontation.

In the closing section of his Second Inaugural Address

Lincoln called for the country *"to do all"* which would achieve the lofty goals of peace at home and around the world. Down through succeeding generations the phrase *"to do all"* has included immense sacrifice and expenditures of life and property. Men and women of the United States Armed Forces and their families have paid much of it. Investments of time, energy, finances, and other assets from the military and those who support them are too numerous to recount. To all those who have dedicated themselves to achieving and preserving unity, freedom, and peace, I offer my sincere thanks.

It is understood that war is expensive. What is perhaps not as clearly understood is the cost of its conclusion. Effects linger beyond bullets and grow as time passes. Conducting and concluding conflicts bear responsibilities for many: the soldier, the family, the caregiver, the society. Many of these obligations are not known and understood, let alone met, until residual effects are revealed over the years.

Organizations exist whose sole purpose is to provide essential care for veterans and their families in vast arenas: mental, social, environmental, physical, spiritual, educational, and emotional. Heretofore unknown maladies have been uncovered as soldiers return from conflicts and try to acclimate into former environments with family, friends, and associates. The difficulties these warriors face are not easily addressed; seldom are they even fully understood.

As society continues to strive to meet necessary and expanding obligations surrounding returning veterans, a stark understanding emerges: there are far more needs and requests to be addressed than there are resources to treat them adequately.

Lincoln's desire to create a just end to his conflict, on behalf of a united country, formed the beginning of a long, arduous, yet worthwhile journey of restoration for the United States of America. That journey continues. Those who walk its paths have not yet reached their final destination. Many would say that this journey is its destination, for no victory in any battle can claim ultimate victory over war's residual aftermath.

A just peace at home and with other countries must be founded upon, and will be secured by, enduring principles and the people who abide by them. The word *lasting* connotes endurance despite the odds arrayed in opposition. Principles endure because their internal strength originates from unadulterated truth. Lasting principles, those over which necessary conflicts are waged and won, become beacons that shed light on how to end well the occurrence of war and protect what endures beyond the battle's close.

It is on the strength of agreement and adherence to abiding principles that a just peace can be established at home and with other nations. Only upon that basis can any goal of peace be realized and maintained. Leaders who desire to achieve these goals build upon agreements anchored upon these principles.

While our nation has withstood countless tests to its resilience, the price of obtaining and cherishing enduring peace will yet be paid again by soldiers of today and tomorrow because it must. The cycle of protecting a free and united land never ceases. The journey is the destination for all who love and cherish liberty, unity, peace, and brotherhood.

The last sentence of Lincoln's inauguration speech begins with this phrase, *"With malice toward none; with charity for all..."* This is the context in which wars are to be concluded. Where peaceful coexistence is desired beyond a war's devastation this is the framework in which to construct a conclusion to a conflict. Though its creation and implementation may surpass human understanding, this is the environment in which healing can occur for societies and leaders who seek to establish and cherish *"a just, and a lasting peace"* for all.

Lessons of War

One Nation under God

I pledge allegiance to the flag of the United States of America, and to the republic for which it stands, one nation under God, indivisible, with liberty and justice for all.

This version of the Pledge of Allegiance was created and adopted in 1954 during the administration of President Dwight D. Eisenhower. Use of the phrase "under God" was not new. Lincoln used the phrase in the Gettysburg Address. In his Second Inaugural Address Lincoln referred to God numerous times. From an historical perspective and enduring precedent the inclusion of the phrase in the pledge to our flag is right and proper.

God is a part of the history of the United States of America. None can study the consequential events that framed the country, and the prevailing beliefs that sustained it, without recognizing a fundamental acceptance of and reliance upon the existence, authority, and will of God. Leaders whose acts formed the destiny of the nation often declared their recognition of and dependence upon God. George Washington, Thomas Jefferson, Benjamin Franklin, Abraham Lincoln, Julia Ward Howe, Susan B. Anthony, Clara Barton, Franklin Roosevelt, John F. Kennedy, Ronald Reagan, and George Bush are examples.

Glen Aubrey

Our nation's national anthem, "The Star-Spangled Banner" references and reveres God. The lyrics of the song were written by Francis Scott Key in 1814. The melody, according to the website, http://www.contemplator.com/america/ssbanner.html, "...was first published in England circa 1780 as *To Anacreon in Heaven*. The melody was probably written by British composer John Stafford Smith."

Most people in the United States are familiar with the first verse. All the verses are memorable. Note particularly the references to the motto of the United States in the fourth verse.

The Star-Spangled Banner
By Francis Scott Key, 1814

Oh, say can you see by the dawn's early light
What so proudly we hailed
at the twilight's last gleaming?
Whose broad stripes and bright stars
thru the perilous fight,
O'er the ramparts we watched
were so gallantly streaming?
And the rocket's red glare, the bombs bursting in air,
Gave proof through the night
that our flag was still there.
Oh, say does that star-spangled banner yet wave
O'er the land of the free
and the home of the brave?

Lessons of War

On the shore, dimly seen
through the mists of the deep,
Where the foe's haughty host
in dread silence reposes,
What is that which the breeze,
o'er the towering steep,
As it fitfully blows, half conceals, half discloses?
Now it catches the gleam
of the morning's first beam,
In full glory reflected now shines in the stream:
'Tis the star-spangled banner! Oh long may it wave
O'er the land of the free
and the home of the brave!

And where is that band
who so vauntingly swore
That the havoc of war
and the battle's confusion,
A home and a country
should leave us no more!
Their blood has washed out
their foul footsteps' pollution.
No refuge could save
the hireling and slave
From the terror of flight,
or the gloom of the grave:

And the star-spangled banner in triumph doth wave
O'er the land of the free
and the home of the brave!

Oh! thus be it ever,
when freemen shall stand
Between their loved home
and the war's desolation!
Blest with victory and peace,
may the heav'n rescued land
Praise the Power that hath made
and preserved us a nation.
Then conquer we must,
when our cause it is just,
And this be our motto:
"In God is our trust."
And the star-spangled banner in triumph shall wave
O'er the land of the free
and the home of the brave!

That Lincoln believed in God and assented to the will of God, there is no doubt. That he encouraged others to consider their responsibilities in light of that dependence is also clearly evident. His leadership model was one of belief in a right cause and dependence upon a just God.

Lincoln's leadership restored the Union. Incidents at

Lessons of War

Gettysburg and those that followed until the close of the war dramatically proved the efficacy of his leadership and the principles he espoused. In all of these, his dependence upon God was evident. This truth will not be denied, because it can't be.

In his Second Inaugural Address the president framed a course for concluding well the war that had been thrust upon him. The contest that ravaged the country had provided the context for his remarks. Lincoln's words resonated throughout our devastated land and pointed the way to restoration and unity.

Events that had occurred at Gettysburg in 1863 also provided a frame of reference for his speech. At that crucial turning point, mid-way through the conflict, Lincoln had delivered the Gettysburg Address. This speech had constructed a course, as well—one for the nation to understand its history and ultimately fulfill its destiny.

The leadership principles of both speeches live because they embody eternal truths. These ideals applied when Lincoln first used them and they apply now. They can be employed in all circumstances of conflict, or of war. The question is never if they will work. The question is: "Does the leader have enough fortitude to use them to achieve a just, and a lasting peace?"

Wars occur as a part of human experience and ultimately cease. Conflicts arise and eventually conclude. Lincoln's Second Inaugural Address contains formulas for enduring, conquering, and ending them well. His formulas were founded upon high and lofty principles that have no end. They are available to any leader who faces disruption and disunity, who desires to achieve meritorious results.

It is up to each leader, regardless of status or station, to embrace and choose the right manners of conducting and concluding war. At the very least these manners illustrate perseverance for a righteous cause, dependence on God, and adherence to eternal law.

You may be the leader or you may aspire to become one. You are encouraged to consider carefully the processes of leadership that Lincoln chose and demonstrated. You are also invited to lead the way he did. The results you obtain may indeed unify opposing parties, establish freedom of communication and commerce, reestablish hope, secure lasting peace, and demonstrate the eternal values of human dignity, determination, mutual respect, and love.

Beneath

Underlined, underscored foundations,
Formed of more than fortune's wishes,
Remain immovable when tried.

Veterans' epitaphs
Fair to behold mid rows of markers
Etch service, birth, conflict, death.

War consumes
While causes for which conflicts rage
Push victorious and enduring ones to pause and reflect.

Lessons of War

Beneficiaries comprehend mere fragments of the magnitude
    of sacrifice,
Accept monumental relinquishments of the dearest of gifts
    on altars of belief
Where ideas born of idealism are fixed upon stone forever.

From *Freedom Light—Expressions of Hope and Evidence* © 2009 Glen Aubrey. Used with permission.

Bibliography

Alleman, Mrs. Tillie (Pierce). *At Gettysburg or What a Girl Saw and Heard of the Battle—A True Narrative.* Baltimore: Butternut and Blue, 1987, 1994. Gettysburg: Stan Clark Military Books, 1987, 1994.

Aubrey, Glen. *Core Teams Work Their Principles and Practices.* San Diego: Creative Team Publishing, 2007.

Aubrey, Glen. *Freedom Light—Expressions of Hope and Evidence.* San Diego: Creative Team Publishing, 2009.

Aubrey, Glen. *Industrial Strength Solutions Build Successful Work Teams!* Frederick: PublishAmerica, 2006.

Aubrey, Glen. *Leadership Is—How to Build Your Legacy*. San Diego: Creative Team Publishing, 2011.

Aubrey, Glen. *Lincoln, Leadership and Gettysburg—Defining Moments of Greatness*. San Diego: Creative Team Publishing, 2009.

Chamberlain, General Joshua Lawrence. *Through Blood and Fire at Gettysburg: General Joshua L. Chamberlain and the 20th Maine*. Gettysburg: Stan Clark Military Books, 1994.

Chamberlain, Joshua Lawrence. *Passing of the Armies: An Account of the Final Campaign of the Army of the Potomac Based upon Personal Reminiscences of the Fifth Army Corps*. Lincoln: University of Nebraska Press, 1998.

Grant, Lieutenant-General Ulysses S. *Personal Memoirs of Ulysses S. Grant*. New York: Webster and Co., 1885, 1886.

Grant, Lieutenant-General Ulysses S. *Report of Lieut. Gen. Ulysses S. Grant, U.S. Army, commanding Armies of the United States, The Richmond (Virginia) Campaign. The Official Records of the War of the Rebellion: a Compilation of the Official Records of the Union and Confederate Armies*. Washington: Government Printing Office, 1880-1901.

Johnson, M.D., F. C., ed. *The Historical Record, A Quarterly Publication Devoted Principally To The Early History of Wyoming Valley With Notes and Quotes, Biographical, Antiquarian, Genealogical. January, 1888, Volume II, No. 1*. Wilkes-Barre: Press of the Wilkes-Barre Record, MDCCCLXXXVIII.

Johnson, Robert Underwood, and Buel, Clarence Clough, eds. *Battles and Leaders of the Civil War, Volume I, Being For The Most Part Contributions By Union and Confederate Officers., Based Upon "The Century War Series."* New York: The Century Company, 1884-1887.

Pitzer, John E. *The Three Days at Gettysburg*. Gettysburg: "News" Press, circa 1900.

Roy, Paul L. *The Last Reunion of the Blue and Gray*. Gettysburg: The Bookmart, 1950.

The Holy Bible Authorized King James Version. London and New York: Collins' Clear-Type Press, 1956.

Acknowledgements

The men who endorsed this book represent untold numbers of warriors and patriots who have sacrificed for the good of the nation they love. Every veteran and soldier of the United States Armed Forces deserves our admiration, accolades, and appreciation.

I acknowledge these men and women. To those who have served or are serving our country I say a heartfelt "Thank You." Your deeds are not unnoticed; your valor is never forgotten.

On the contrary, the people of today remember your contributions perhaps more than ever. Events at the opening of the 21st Century demonstrated once again that America remains the target of misguided and evil individuals who seek to overthrow and undermine the country that has wrought the greatest good in the world. The selfishness and radical commitments of these terrorists know no bounds. Their goal appears to be to subjugate or eliminate others who do not possess world and religious ideologies similar or identical to their own. Their cruel and cowardly methods simply show how far people who don't understand freedom will go to destroy the basis of *"a just, and a lasting peace, among ourselves, and with all nations."*

Attacks and threats of attacks will continue. Conflicts will never cease. Wars, though fought very differently than before, will still be waged. America must continue to be vigilant.

To those charged with protecting our freedom, I offer my unadulterated support. The United States Armed Forces are guarantors of life, liberty, and the pursuit of happiness for many, and will continue to be thus because these men and women are part of *We the People*. They *are* us.

I also offer my sincere appreciation to those who directly contributed to the success of this book: Justin Aubrey, Deanna Christiansen, and Jordan Trementozzi. Their labors helped make the book come to life.

Finally, I want to offer my appreciation to my mother, Zela Aubrey, who passed away in 2011. During August of 2011, I was privileged to read the manuscript of *Lessons of War—Lincoln's Second Inaugural Address, Leadership at Gettysburg* to her at her residential care facility. She was attentive, engaged, and so appreciative of the time and content. Mom: our family will miss you. Thanks for your support of my writing endeavors.

The Author

Glen Aubrey is President and CEO of Creative Team Resources Group, Inc. (CTRG), www.ctrg.com. He is a business consultant, conference speaker, leadership trainer, author, music writer and orchestrator, and poet. He has authored *Leadership Is—How to Build Your Legacy*, *Industrial Strength Solutions Build Successful Work Teams!*, *Core Teams Work Their Principles and Practices*, *Growing Core Teams*, *Core Team Impact!*, *Go From the Night—Journeys of Thought*, *Meditations on Life*, *Arranging Notes*, *L.E.A.D.—Learning, Education, Action, Destiny* and its study guide *Leadership Works*, *Freedom Light—Expressions of Hope and Evidence*, *Lincoln, Leadership and Gettysburg—Defining Moments of Greatness*, and *Lessons of War—Lincoln's Second Inaugural Address, Leadership at Gettysburg*.

You are invited to visit these websites:
    www.ctrg.com
    www.CreativeTeamPublishing.com
    www.LeadershipIs.com

www.Industrial-Strength-Solutions.com
www.CoreTeamsWork.com
www.Lead52.com
www.Lincoln-Leadership-Gettysburg.com
www.LessonsOfWar.com
www.GoFromTheNight.com
www.Freedom-Light.com
www.glenaubrey.com

Creative Team Resources Group, Inc. (CTRG)

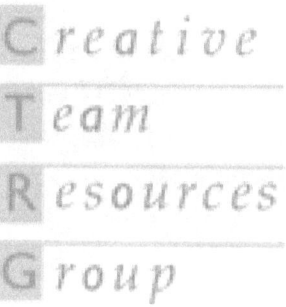

www.ctrg.com
www.LeadershipIs.com
www.Industrial-Strength-Solutions.com
www.CoreTeamsWork.com
www.Lead52.com
www.Lincoln-Leadership-Gettysburg.com
www.LessonsOfWar.com

CTRG provides quality resources for the development of teams within organizations whose desires are to grow and develop their personnel and achieve greater results in product or service provision. CTRG gives people great information that allows them to make changes in how they live and work and does this through building core teams. Our resources include conferences, consultation, and coaching.

Our foundational principle is that people are more important than production and relationships precede and give definition to function. The value of a person's contributions comes from that person's inherent worth. The value of the person causes the contributions a person makes to achieve even greater results.

Contact CTRG at the websites above. We will demonstrate first-hand how our team building principles can work for you. Glen Aubrey, President and CEO, along with other CTRG staff are available to your group for speaking engagements, on-site training and leadership coaching. CTRG looks forward to serving and working with you!

Creative Team Publishing (CTP)

Creative Team Publishing (CTP, www.CreativeTeamPublishing.com) is a division of Creative Team Resources Group, Inc. (CTRG, www.ctrg.com). CTP was formed in 2007 to publish and distribute business and team development, leadership training, and poetry books, as well as literature of inspiration, insight, human achievement, and positive general interest.

The company's commitment is to make high quality literature available, and engage in excellence throughout the process of publication. Customer satisfaction is a top priority. Because CTP practices due diligence in selecting which books it will publish, CTP chooses to work with authors and contributors who meet a qualified standard of literary competence and uplifting content.

CTP is a fee-for-service publisher. Products offered include the following:

Pre-Press
1. Editing
2. Proofing
3. Revision
4. Typesetting
5. Four Color Cover Design
6. ISBN
7. Print Set-up

Post-Press
1. Product supply
2. Press releases

Contact Creative Team Publishing. Please visit our company website, www.CreativeTeamPublishing.com for information. We look forward to reviewing your literary creation.

Books by Glen Aubrey

Order these books at the websites below or from
www.CreativeTeamPublishing.com.

Leadership Is—How to Build Your Legacy
www.LeadershipIs.com

Industrial Strength Solutions Build Successful Work Teams!
www.Industrial-Strength-Solutions.com

Core Teams Work Their Principles and Practices
www.CoreTeamsWork.com

L.E.A.D.—Learning, Education, Action, Destiny and
Leadership Works—Advanced Study Guide for L.E.A.D.
www.Lead52.com

Lincoln, Leadership and Gettysburg—Defining Moments of Greatness
www.Lincoln-Leadership-Gettysburg.com

Lessons of War—Lincoln's Second Inaugural Address, Leadership at Gettysburg
www.LessonsOfWar.com

Go From the Night—Journeys of Thought, Meditations on Life
www.GoFromTheNight.com

Freedom Light—Expressions of Hope and Evidence
www.Freedom-Light.com

Growing Core Teams
www.CreativeTeamPublishing.com

Core Team Impact!
www.CreativeTeamPublishing.com

Arranging Notes
www.CreativeMusicEnterprises.com

Music Audio Recordings by Glen Aubrey

Order these recordings from www.CreativeMusicEnterprises.com or from www.CreativeTeamPublishing.com.

Go From the Night Meditation
Glen Aubrey Solo Piano
Pat Kelley Guitars
Narratives

Meditation
Glen Aubrey Solo Piano
Pat Kelley Guitars

Timeless
Glen Aubrey Solo Piano

Legacy
Glen Aubrey Piano and Orchestra

Beautiful, A Symphonic Experience
Music by Lindamarie Todd and
Glen Aubrey

Born Is the King
Christmas Keyboard Reflections

The Custom Album
Piano Solos by Glen Aubrey

Reflecting Hymn
The Rock Album
Piano Solos by Glen Aubrey
Vocal "There Is A Redeemer" by Steve Duff

What Child Is This?
Glen Aubrey Solo Piano

www.ingramcontent.com/pod-product-compliance
Lightning Source LLC
Chambersburg PA
CBHW022016290426
44109CB00015B/1194